PROTEUS

Studies in English Literature

TO MY WIFE

PROTEUS
STUDIES IN ENGLISH LITERATURE

D. S. Brewer

D. S. BREWER

First published 1958
The Kenkyusha Press, Tokyo

Reprinted in Paperback 2009
D. S. Brewer, Cambridge

Transferred to digital printing

ISBN 978-1-84384-205-7

D. S. Brewer is an imprint of Boydell & Brewer Ltd
PO Box 9, Woodbridge, Suffolk IP12 3DF, UK
and of Boydell & Brewer Inc.
668 Mt Hope Avenue, Rochester, NY 14620, USA
website: www.boydellandbrewer.com

A CiP catalogue record for this book is available
from the British Library

This publication is printed on acid-free paper

PREFACE

The substance of this book is based on lectures which I have given in Japan while on leave from the University of Birmingham, England. I should like to express here my gratitude to all those scholars and students in Japan who have listened to me with such patience, and whose interest in English literature has been so stimulating to me.

It is impossible to name all the people to whom I have been indebted, but I should particularly like to mention Dr. Takeshi Saito for his help in making this book possible. I am also very much indebted to the publishers and printers, not only for their customary skill and care, but for the forbearance with which they received a late manuscript and the speed with which they have published it.

A foreigner these days in Japan receives much generous treatment from his Japanese colleagues and assistants which it is difficult to repay. And he receives everywhere in Japan from brief acquaintances or unknown persons—from the parents or relatives of Japanese friends, from shopkeepers, taxi-drivers, maids, strangers

[v]

in trains, passers-by in the street—many of the

> . . . little, nameless, unremembered, acts
> Of kindness and of love,

which, Wordsworth says, make up ' that best portion
of a good man's life ', and for which it is often enough
difficult even to express one's thanks.   As a small token
of the appreciation which I and my family have felt,
any royalties this book may earn will be paid into a
scholarship fund for Japanese students in need of
financial help.

D. S. BREWER

The International Christian
University
20 June 1958

CONTENTS

CONVENTION IN ENGLISH LITERATURE

I.	A Statement of Themes: Difference, Change, Similarity, Relativity, Interpretation ...	1
II.	Custom and Convention	6
III.	Convention and Reality	9
IV.	Change and Continuity	20
V.	The Sense of Time	23
VI.	The Love-story	36
VII.	Character	45
VIII.	Class-distinctions	50
IX.	Religion and Morality	57
X.	General Comments	66

THE HUMOUR OF CHAUCER: THE ARTIST AS INSIDER

I.	The Nature of Humour	69
II.	"The Book of the Duchess"	77
III.	"The House of Fame"	78
IV.	"The Parliament of Fowls"	89
V.	"The Canterbury Tales"	102
VI.	Humour and Poetry	129

SHAKESPEARE AND THE IMMORTALITY OF THE SOUL 133

ASPECTS OF NATURE AND WORDSWORTH
    I. The European Nature 156
    II. Nature and History in the Eighteenth Century 163
    III. Wordsworth 174

E. M. FORSTER AND SAWSTON: THE DIVIDED MIND 198

THE MODERN ENGLISH LITERARY TEMPER AND THE CRISIS OF EXPANSION 233

The business of art is to reveal the relation between man and his circumambient universe, at the living moment. As mankind is always struggling in the toils of old relationships, art is always ahead of the times, which themselves are far in the rear of the living moment.

—D. H. Lawrence, *Phoenix*, p. 527.

. . . even art is utterly dependent on philosophy; or, if you prefer it, on a metaphysic. The metaphysic may not be anywhere very accurately stated, and may be quite unconscious in the artist, yet it is a metaphysic that governs men all the time.

—D. H. Lawrence, Preface to *Fantasia*.

Our education from the start has *taught* us a certain range of emotions, what to feel and what not to feel, and how to feel the feelings we allow ourselves to feel.

—D. H. Lawrence, *Sex, Literature and Censorship*, p. 233.

CONVENTION IN ENGLISH LITERATURE

I

A Statement of Themes: Difference, Change, Similarity, Relativity, Interpretation

To read old books, to read foreign books, and to live in a foreign country are three experiences that have much in common. Whether we travel in space or time, to make it worth while we must travel in imagination also, as we contemplate with pleasure or dislike but always with interest the infinite variety of humankind. We are always being surprised, always entranced by new possibilities, always lured on by the possibilities of new understanding of life. We need never be bored; we shall come to the end of our own lives long before we finish exploring the diversities of life.

Now and again, however, we shall like to pause, as a man pauses on the top of a mountain, looking back over the towns, fields, lakes, he has already crossed, looking over their general outline, as they extend towards the vague blue line of the infinite sea from which he has come and to which he will return. The impulse to consider a little, to codify one's impressions, map out the land, is as strong as the desire to seek new countries, new experiences, more and different books.

The chief impressions the traveller will be conscious of, as he looks back over the way he has come, is the paradox of the immense diversity and astonishing similarity of human experience.   If we assert either the difference or the similarity of human experience without the other we distort the truth.   Difference and similarity are usually obvious enough, yet such is our natural inertia that each needs constant emphasis and above all, constant definition.   Half the world's troubles today spring from the incapacity of each nation to discover in what ways it is different from and similar to its friends and its enemies.

There is no fact more obvious than difference between two cultures, or between various ages of the same culture, and none we more constantly disregard.   In a foreign country we interpret behaviour, however ' odd ', as if it were motivated by exactly the same concepts and sensibilities as would lie behind such behaviour in our own country.   The reader of a foreign literature has a perpetual tendency to treat it as a distorted variant of his own.   We often simply fail to notice deep differences because our minds supply familiar elements if they are not present, or fail to register unfamiliar elements.   Or again, in reading very old or very new books, we often condemn them as incompetent attempts at something familiar, and fail to recognise that they are perhaps successfully achieving something strange.   Literary history provides many examples of this : in our own day Mr. Eliot's *Waste Land* and many of the novels of D. H. Lawrence have been celebrated victims.   Ancient or foreign literature suffers in the same way as new literature, though less spectacularly.   Because ideas and feelings have changed, meanings are read into an old author that he could never have known, or demands are unconsciously made upon him that he never intended to satisfy; and the insight and enjoyment he provides are neglected because we no longer automatically expect them. Our minds, which should be windows, are darkened by idleness and turn into mirrors. We look out and see only what is already within.

In literature we are especially liable to neglect the differences that exist between the writings of one age and those of another. The superficial differences may strike the eye as a kind of quaintness, but we easily assume without thinking that the basic presuppositions and feelings about life are the same in other periods as in ours. This is a great pity. It leads to gross mis-understanding, it deprives us of much interest and pleasure, it contradicts the whole purpose of our reading. We have to remind ourselves again of what we already know; or rather we have to give imaginative life to what usually remains a dead concept: that things change. We know that we ourselves are different from what we were last year: that we differ in thought and feeling from our parents, that they so differed from themselves and from their parents. The constant change indeed gives rise to both the pleasure and the necessity for reading older literature, just as from it arises, as Mr. Eliot has recently said, the necessity of writing new literature. Our presuppositions, feelings, ideas, change steadily. We need continually to test and perhaps re-imagine those of the past, just as we need to create, or have created for us, the works of literature which minister to those of the present.

In order to appreciate difference and change we must

believe in cultural relativity. To do this we must abandon any assumption that our own presuppositions, feelings and ideas are the norm of all human experience. This is most difficult to do, though it is as vital that we should do it for the sake of our future as it is for the sake of understanding and making use of the past. We must accept our own attitudes and beliefs as relative to our present time, we must impose them neither on the past nor on the future. Everyone would agree to this in considering the laws of science. We must also agree to this relativity in matters of religion, morals, manners, art; in all departments of life. Whether we like it or not, change is irresistible, difference inevitable; it is the law of life. To insist on cultural relativity is only to recognise the essential condition of life, and to enable ourselves to live more adequately. Again this is no more than to state the obvious, and again we see the obvious neglected everywhere, in common beliefs and behaviour, in literary criticism, in national and international politics. The practical issue of a belief in cultural relativity is toleration, and toleration can hardly be supposed to be in excessive supply today.

Yet although we must recognise constant change and pervasive differences in human experience, we must not deny the fundamental similarity of human nature at all times and places within our present knowledge. Could constant change be recognised if there were not something permanent to compare it with? For all the changes and differences among human beings, there is also a continuing basis of comparison, as there is of sympathy, in our common physical structure, our common biological and psychological necessities. The doctrine of 'the unchanging human heart' is an absurdity, but at least it reminds us that we each have a heart. We always have something in common with other men, however noble or criminal, however near or remote in time and place. Experience and various authorities, however else they differ, assure us that in some sense all men are brothers.

Difference and similarity give each other meaning in human affairs. Without difference we should be undifferentiated, unconscious of ourselves. Without similarity we should be unconscious of anyone but ourselves, for we could not enter with imaginative sympathy into other lives. The appreciation of difference and similarity is the function—as it is the delight—of literature ; the literature both of our times, and of the past, just as it is the delight of foreign travel. But the delight must depend on our willingness to accept both difference and similarity—though sometimes it is the similarity which alarms us, as well as the difference.

It is the similarities between us as human beings that make the differences so interesting, and make it possible to hope to understand them, at least in part. But what we must not hope to do is to strip off the differences until we come to the similarities, as if differences were merely suits of clothes, and we were all much the same ' natural ' men underneath. There is no such thing as a ' natural ' man in this sense. Our differences are as much a part of our true selves as our similarities. We can never become the same as each other. People, literatures, cultures, differ and resemble each other as languages do. Japanese and English are two totally different languages. They have no common factor between them, no basic similarity, no linguistic sediment, which would remain when all differences have been removed. Yet it is perfectly possible for one language to be translated into the other, perfectly possible for people to be bilingual. No doubt in the process of translation much is lost. One who is ignorant of Japanese will never taste the full flavour of Japanese literature and life. But enough can be translated to extend his imagination as it could never be extended by English literature and life. Different human feelings and thoughts can be transferred—admittedly not completely—from one language to the other, although there is no common linguistic factor. So from one culture to another, or from one stage of the same culture to another, different thoughts and feelings can be translated, not by abandoning differences, but by accepting and interpreting them. Our common humanity makes this possible, even though common humanity is not something which can be extracted from life as its essence. Our common humanity, in all its different manifestations, makes possible, desirable, and interesting, the reading of old books, the reading of foreign books, and the experience of foreign countries.

II

Custom and Convention

' No man is an Iland, intire of itself ' : we are made by our environments, and one of the ways in which our differences and similarities appear is in our individual responses to the general pressures of the time. The general pressure is much the same for everybody : we differ in our personal responses. Each human being is a result of the impact of the pressure of the whole culture upon his initial naked human potential. In dealing with a whole culture the pressure which is exerted upon the individual person can best be understood as the force of custom.

> The fact of first-rate importance is the predominant role that custom plays in experience and in belief, and the very great varieties it may manifest.
> No man ever looks at the world with pristine eyes. He sees it edited by a definite set of customs and institutions and ways of thinking. Even in his philosophical probings he cannot go behind these stereotypes ; his very concepts of the true and false will still have reference to his particular traditional customs. . . . The life history of the individual is first and foremost an accommodation to the patterns and standards traditionally handed down in his community. From the moment of his birth the customs into which he is born shape his experience and behaviour. By the time he can talk, he is the little creature of his culture, and by the time he is grown and able to take part in its activities, its habits are his habits, its beliefs are his beliefs, its impossibilities are his impossibilities. . . . There is no social problem it is more incumbent upon us to understand than this of the role of custom. Until we are intelligent as to its laws and varieties, the main complicating facts of human life must remain unintelligible.

(Ruth Benedict, *Patterns of Culture*, 1934, Chapter I)

The function and extent of custom in our lives have had to wait long for recognition.

> There is another circumstance that has made the serious study of custom a late and often a half-heartedly pursued discipline. . . . Custom did not challenge the attention of social theorists because it was the very stuff of their own thinking : it was the lens without which they could not see at all. Precisely in proportion as it was fundamental, it had its existence outside the field of conscious attention.   (ibid. Chapter I)

The study of literature can learn much from the study of anthropology, for literature offers a world or culture of its own, derived from ' real life ' indeed, but separate and autonomous too. Custom in ' real life ' corresponds to convention in literature.

The idea of convention in literature is as commonplace as that of custom in life. But like custom, the literary convention has been understood in far too superficial and local a sense, and still awaits full recognition and proper study. By convention we should understand not merely stock literary devices but the whole habit of thought and feeling which informs a mass of literature of one particular time, or of one particular culture. A convention is the way of looking at something, and the way of rendering it in art, which is inherited by any particular person. The sum total of conventions is the general world-view which a writer derives from his history and his times. It is his framework, his starting point. The writer like everyone else *learns* his most ' natural ' feelings and thoughts. The convention is not to be despised because it is not original with the writer. There is very little in any man that can be original. The convention represents normal human thought and feeling at one time, or even, in one culture, over a period of time.

This is not to say that the convention never changes. It may remain static for long periods, or change only slightly; but change it must. The reason that a convention changes is because, in order to be realised at all, it must unite with the potentiality of the individual human being, and since every human being is slightly different, there is continually a slight modification of the convention. The convention a man receives from his father he cannot help altering, however slightly, by living it : so that it comes to his son in slightly different form. Change is of the nature of life. We learn how to feel and think, but we never learn our lesson properly, and so the lesson we pass on is different from the one we have received. Furthermore, we sometimes deliberately alter the conventions we have received, when we feel they are no longer adequate.

III

Convention and Reality

Convention should be regarded as the accepted mode of thought and feeling, and hence of behaviour. It is not merely superficial, but governs our deepest thoughts and feelings as well as the social behaviour to which the word is usually restricted. Literary conventions are the representation in literature of conventions in the wider sense, as well as the comparatively trivial literary devices to which the word is usually restricted.

Convention in its wider sense governs all our activities. The laws of science are conventions of thought, and they provide a useful example of convention because being less personal they are more easily considered in a detached way. We see how they change. In the Middle Ages the force of gravity was understood as the ' love ' which bound all things together. Galileo and Newton substituted progressively different concepts of the phenomenon of a piece of matter falling to the earth. Einstein has presumably substituted another concept. These concepts are conventions for approaching ' reality ', whatever that may be. A convention when new seems always to express reality completely, and often claims to be reality itself. But as human experience accumulates, so the convention becomes less and less adequate, until a new one is evolved. It usually takes a man of genius to perceive that the old convention is really inadequate, and to replace it by a more adequate convention.

The mistake that is usually made is to suppose that the older convention was ' merely ' a convention, and that the newer convention is actual truth, and that we have now come face to face with reality. History easily shows how false this is. We can never escape from convention and arrive at an absolute naked truth outside ourselves. To change from Newton's law to Einstein's may very well be an improvement, but it is also merely a change from one convention to another.

Scientific laws are very simple conventions because they engage chiefly one part of the mind, and deal with a very restricted area of human experience. Conventions which deal with what is less easily measurable and which involve very complicated thoughts and feelings are less easily defined. A good historical example is provided by the present controversy over the ' demythologisation ' of the Gospels, started by the work of Rudolph Bultmann. Bultmann seems to assume that the writers of the Gospels and their predecessors interpreted what they knew of the life of Christ in accordance with their natural ' mythological ' way of thinking, and that consequently they misinterpreted it. There has therefore been an attempt to get rid of the ' mythological ' element of the Gospels, and arrive at the ' real ' truth of the life of Christ. The danger here lies in assuming that one can peel off the mythological aspects like a suit of clothes. If the Gospels are ' demythologised ' it can only be by substituting our own mythology, that is, our own convention. This might be an improvement for us, if properly done : but the modern account so arrived at would be quite as much a conventional one as the ancient account was.

If reality is for the moment thought of as something external, convention is the means by which the human being gets to grips with reality. It is as if convention were the knife-and-fork, the chopsticks, with which the food, reality, is eaten. If we use neither knife-and-fork, nor chopsticks, but our fingers, we are not thereby escaping convention, we are reverting to a more primitive convention. Our experience can only be apprehended *through* conventions, though it is not composed *of* conventions.

When thinking of the individual person, convention may appear in two ways. When we think of the way the individual person learns, convention appears as the general force which forms his mind and thought. We learn the form of our emotions just as we learn our alphabet. But when we think of the formed individual's response to external reality, convention appears as his own personal, though learnt, way of responding to reality. There is really a kind of triangle of forces composed of the individual, convention, and reality. What makes the situation so interesting is that convention always claims to be a representation of reality, and may in fact be as near to such reality, whatever it may be, as we can hope to get. For the most part in our ordinary lives we naturally assume that convention truly represents reality, and we assume that convention and reality are the same. But they never are, there is always something unaccounted for. This is presumably why it is possible to go on changing and improving the conventions, that is, the laws, of science. There is, so to speak, a gap between convention and reality. This continual gap between convention and reality, which at certain periods in history is very slight, and at others, like the present, is in many subjects very wide, is what causes us continually to labour at the sciences, and is also what continuously demands the writing of new literature and the fresh understanding of old.

A great poet, or novelist, or dramatist, may be said to close, or at least to narrow, the gap between convention and reality for his own time ; that is, he changes the convention so as to bring it into accord with reality.

What he in fact does is to establish a newer, more satisfactory convention, and there will inevitably come a time
when because of the ceaseless change of human life our
feelings and perceptions of what is real will differ from
the convention by which we are accustomed to approach
reality (whatever that may be). How this happens
would be difficult to say. We may say either that a
convention makes us aware of its own inadequacy
through some self-evident inconsistency or other failure,
the inadequacy arising from change in ourselves or
perhaps in our environment ; or we may say that we
may have some direct perception or intuition of the
outer world extending beyond the range of convention.
Perhaps both are true. For the present discussion the
failure of convention, rather than its causes, is important. At all events, conventions do become inadequate, after being felt to be adequate, and it is the
mark of a genius both to perceive the failure of the
old convention and, especially, to create a new. In
the field of the physical sciences this was Newton's and
Einstein's supreme achievement. In literature the process is excellently illustrated in the changes in poetic
diction, especially those initiated by Wordsworth and
Mr. Eliot. In each case it was felt that the ' language
of poetry' had strayed too far from the language of
' real ' life. We are now in a position to say that what
Wordsworth and Mr. Eliot substituted for an outmoded
poetic diction was equally a poetic diction ; a convention
of the kind of language to be used in poetry. In each
case the new convention was both necessary and successful in approximating to reality, even if Wordsworth

himself lost his grip on his own new convention and in later life largely relapsed into the old.

When the old convention no longer represents or no longer seems to be identified with reality, it must be scrapped. It is no longer useful to the working poet or scientist. It is however a matter of common experience that literature which has already been written does not suffer in quite the way we should expect. Literature written in an outworn convention is by no means itself necessarily outworn. Here we must emphasise the distinction between the working poet or novelist or dramatist and the apparently non-creative writer or critic. This obvious distinction is often badly misunderstood, especially in England. Addison remarks somewhere that it is absurd to criticise someone else who is doing what one cannot do oneself. There is often a tendency in England to suggest that poetry, for example, can only be truly criticised by poets. There are many obvious arguments against this view, and we need not pause to refute it again. But it is a fact that the greatest critics of English literature in England have all been great poets: Sidney, Dryden, Johnson, Coleridge, Arnold, Mr. Eliot. Such a state of affairs would be well worth further discussion, for which there is no space here. What should be pointed out is that until some poetry by Aristotle and Sainte-Beuve (to mention only two) is discovered, and found to be great poetry, we must regard the English situation as a cultural oddity, and we need not take too seriously those who say that the best critics *must* be practitioners of the art they criticise.

We must distinguish between two kinds of readers, whom I will call the writing reader and the reading reader. The writing reader is the small class of literary creative writer. He tends to read what is useful to him, or what he thinks will be useful to him, for his own writing. He tends to praise, as again Mr. Eliot points out, what is useful or sympathetic to his own aims, and to ignore or condemn what is not. Thus, at a more flippant level, when we find Mr. Kingsley Amis (a university lecturer in English literature) in a critical *jeu d'esprit* in the *Spectator* in 1957 condemning all English literature except novels, plays, and short poems, we are not surprised to find that he is a highly successful novelist and a writer of excellent short poems ; we may suspect that he will soon write a play. His condemnation of all great poetry except lyrics need not be taken very seriously. The criticism of a practitioner, then, tends to be narrow or even intolerant, but if exercised on a sympathetic subject may well go deep into its achievements in a way impossible to the critic who is not a practitioner.

The critic who is not a practitioner is the reading reader, and his response is likely to be more tolerant and more varied than that of the writing reader. His characteristic weaknesses are lack of intensity of response and of concentration of insight. Yet the reading reader is not merely passive. Like the writing reader he also reads to learn and to use : but he turns what he has learnt into non-literary channels, he uses his reading not to help him formulate and express ideas and feelings as new literature, but to enrich his knowledge and enjoyment of life in general, or to feed other interests like philosophy, psychology, anthropology or the history of literature.

Reading readers are a huge class: they are indeed ' the ordinary readers ', while writing readers are comparatively few. And this is why literature based on outdated conventions of thought and feeling still appeals. Reading readers are not actively concerned to help evolve current or new conventions in literature. Their concern is, to use Mr. Eliot's phrase, ' to understand and enjoy '. One convention is as good to them as another, though naturally some conventions are more familiar, agreeable, or sympathetic. Such readers are less likely to reject conventions as such, in search of help for their own concerns. Their interests are wider, more philosophical (in the old general sense) than those of the writing reader.

Sometimes a work of literature may serve both classes equally well, as Mr. Eliot's poetry has, and, under his aegis, as Donne's poetry has until quite recently. Some writers, like Shakespeare, seem very rarely to have been of much use to the writing reader (Keats is one of the rare exceptions). Some writers, like Chaucer and Milton and Dryden have exercised a strong influence on writing readers for a hundred years or more, providing a particular tone of voice, a poetic diction, usable conventions. The greatness of a writer cannot be measured in terms of this kind of direct usefulness. For one thing it never lasts very long. For another, I should be prepared to maintain in argument (if not quite certainly to believe) that the *direct* influence of

Chaucer and Milton, to name no more, on succeeding writers, was wholly bad. The greatness of a writer must be measured by his effect on reading readers— that is, by the way he may influence the *whole* tone of feeling and attitude to the world of a reader whose aim is understanding and enjoyment of both art and life— or rather, more truly, of life through art. Of course the distinction I have made between writing readers and reading readers is a little too clear-cut. Most writing readers, that is, most poets, novelists and dramatists, must surely at some time read ' just for pleasure ' without seeking materials and scaffolding for their own new structures. When they so read, they join the great majority who keep a writer's work alive.

It is through the ordinary readers that literature survives. An outdated convention, in literature, is merely another convention ; and a convention, whether of a different age, or of a different contemporary culture, is a way of approaching reality. The realities with which literature is concerned are states of feeling about the nature of human life in the universe, or part of it. They may change, but they do not become outdated. Nothing human should be alien to us, and the art of dead men may still speak to us. ' There is but one society, the noble living and the noble dead.'

That is why literary conventions, great and small, are worth our thought : because until we understand them, we cannot understand the literature which embodies them and which they made possible. In some cases, because we all share some given traits of humanity, and because we rarely stray right outside our own traditions, we can get some pleasure out of an old or foreign author without thinking about or noticing the conventions of his thought, simply because we also share them. It is possible for an Englishman today to enjoy Shakespeare to some extent without any realisation of the force of convention, simply because some of the conventions that govern Shakespeare still govern him. But when he comes across a plot in which Shakespeare is governed by a convention that has now lapsed, the ordinary reader's understanding goes wildly astray, and in consequence his enjoyment wanes, because the action seems unnatural. Such is what usually happens when *Measure for Measure* is played. Since there is little understanding in modern England of the religious sanctions of chastity, and little feeling for the immortality of the soul, it is common to think of Isabella as cold and selfish in refusing to prostitute herself to save her brother's life. With this condemnation of Isabella the whole play is misinterpreted, and the text itself misread and misunderstood. For the same reason most university teachers of English literature will have had the experience of hearing their pupils, young men and women of impeccable morals, describe *Comus*, the most warmly medieval and least puritan of Milton's poems in its feeling for the divine power of chastity, as ' puritanical ', and hence ' ignorant of human nature ', ' harsh ', ' cold ' and ' unnatural '.

What is most noticeable about responses where there has been a failure to understand the convention, is that where understanding is not, enjoyment perishes. With enjoyment fails the will and nerve to explore, and we finish up as nervous readers, bewildered and disgusted by really modern literature, because it begins to differ from our present familiar if inadequate conventions, and equally bewildered and disgusted by older literature, because it also differs from our familiar conventions. So we move in a small parish of time and place, and generalize on the nature of literature from acquaintance with a few works of the immediate past. Our thoughts and feelings petrify in one local and transient form. We are less alive than we could and should be, and we do not know the truth.

Recognition and knowledge of convention alone is not, however, enough, though it is much. The final and most difficult work of literary criticism is to interpret conventions: to show how the conventions of Dante, or Chaucer, or Shakespeare, or any other author, correspond to the conventions of today, so that we may understand the nature of the reality the poet is attempting to describe. That is the most difficult task, which needs both knowledge and sympathy, and a kind of recreative power of its own. There is no formula for it, any more than there is any formula for writing a poem. Indeed, a critic of older literature who aspires to this task almost certainly depends heavily on modern literature for his capacity to enter imaginatively into the conventions of the past. Modern literature must help us interpret older literature: *The Waste Land* must help us with *The Parlement of Foules*. Then we shall also find the reverse process; *The Parlement* adds to our understanding and enjoyment of *The Waste Land*. There is mutual enrichment.

IV

Change and Continuity

English literature is governed, like any other literature, by a number of conventions of varied importance. A few of these I shall now examine, by way of example. The subject demands extensive treatment, but to consider it even on the present small scale may help to add to our understanding and enjoyment of individual authors, and may also help to realise something of the body of English literature as a whole. Just as there is an added interest in one of Shakespeare's lyrics if you know the whole play, and an added interest in the play if you know the others, so there is an added interest and enjoyment in Shakespeare's whole work if you know something of the general body of Elizabethan, and finally English, literature. No doubt such a survey may seem a vast undertaking, but there are sufficient great writers at most periods of English literature to make a broad main road from which the surrounding country—provided you do not go too fast—may be viewed. The authors of *Beowulf, The Wanderer, The Seafarer, The Ancrene Wisse;* Chaucer, Malory, Spenser, Shakespeare, Milton, Dryden, Pope, Samuel Johnson, Wordsworth, Coleridge, Jane Austen, Scott, Dickens, George Eliot, D. H. Lawrence, T. S. Eliot; these are enough to give us a vantage ground. From them we can get a rough picture of dominating conventions in English literature. Without a reasonable knowledge of all these authors, or of closely comparable ones where they exist, any critic of English literature is bound to lack perspective and standards.

There is no question of expecting to find the same qualities in the same proportions and relations in each of the authors I have mentioned. Our first conscious-ness must be that of change and development within the literary culture. This may be illustrated briefly in a trivial matter, half literary and half a part of general behaviour—the weeping of men. In *Beowulf* they weep for great grief or great joy, without excess or restraint. By the fourteenth century it is clear from contemporary chronicles and from the writings of Chaucer that men broke into tears very easily, frequently and copiously. One of the reasons why an unprepared reader finds it hard to appreciate the boldness and goodness of Chaucer's Troilus is that he weeps so much. At this period, as with Malory's in the middle of the fifteenth century, it is clear that the boldest, bravest, toughest knights might weep without being thought cry-babies. There is a change by the end of the sixteenth century. Shake-speare's heroes weep, but they struggle against tears; tears are considered to be a sign of ' the mother ', that is, of feminine weakness in a man. Perhaps some-thing is due here to the actor's difficulty in daylight, barely separated from the nearest of his audience, in actually producing or simulating tears when the moment seems to demand them. But the contemptuous refer-ences to tears are significant. Milton's Satan like-wise fights against his tears, even though they are such as angels weep, and the latter parts of the seventeenth century, and earlier eighteenth appear to have been

comparatively tearless.   With the ' sentimental comedy '
and the sentimental novel of the eighteenth century,
tears once again became fashionable and in the latter part
of the eighteenth century there was something of a cult
of tears, as a sign of sensibility.   Henry Mackenzie's
Man of Feeling (1771) must surely have the most lachry-
mose hero in fiction.   Mr. Pickwick and others can shed
a manly or maudlin tear with ease, but with the reform
of the public schools and the dominance of public school
ideals in the upper middle class, and with this class's
predominance in the country's affairs in the latter part
of the nineteenth century, we come to the current myth
of the Englishman—a stolid, emotionally inhibited person.   The average Englishman today feels it shameful
to weep in public.   Yet persons of strong individuality
break away from the pattern.   Appsley Cherry-Garrard
says that Captain R. F. Scott, the Antarctic explorer,
burst into tears more easily than any other man he had
known: and Sir Winston Churchill's capacity for
shedding a tear on an appropriate occasion is well
known.

It would be easily possible to multiply such examples
of change, especially of the sentiments, and a history of
English sentiment is much to be wished.   When, for
example, did English kindness begin?   The modern
English much pride themselves on this virtue, not without reason.   But Elizabethan Englishmen found much
enjoyment in watching half-a-dozen men whip a blinded
bear, and Sir Philip Sidney says we laugh at cripples.
On the other hand, Elizabethan Englishmen were remarkable for their resolute bravery in the face of death,

and their belief in immortality. It is doubtful if they are so outstanding now.

Many of these are small matters, but they affect our idea of the quality of a nation; they are conventions, and they show remarkable change. But some more general qualities have changed less, and are worth examining.

V

The Sense of Time

One of the chief of these conventions is the concern with time. By no means all cultures and nations share it. The Ancient Greeks, for example, like the Japanese, were unable to work out a satisfactory chronology. The origins of the English and European concern with time are to be found partly in the Judaic sense of time and history expressed in the Old Testament. The Roman Empire and all it represented, its fate and its survival as an ideal, was another important factor. Their union in Augustine's *City of God* gives us perhaps the first attempt to convey a genuine sense of the passage of time. But the English seem to have felt the pressure of hisory particularly strongly. Perhaps it was because from the moment they landed on the shores of Britain, they were surrounded by the monuments of the past— cities of stone, and in the country brick villas. They camped outside the cities rather than enter them—the fine stone town of Chester, for example, lay desolate for centuries after the legions left. Deeper even than this, there seems to have been some temperamental

English quality which led to a contemplation, often touched with mealancholy, of the past. In penitential poems like *The Wanderer* and *The Seafarer* this feeling is turned into devotional channels ; men come, men go : All things remain in God : so love God only. But the feeling is not narrowly devotional. *Beowulf* is remarkable for the long look the Christian author takes into the dark backward and abysm of time, before the true knowledge of Christ, but when men were also heroic. Apart from the poetic symbolism of man and his foes, of youth and victory, age and death, which lies at the centre of the poem, *Beowulf* has a framework of historical allusion which supports and as it were justifies the central myth. *The Anglo-Saxon Chronicle* shows the same feeling for history by its very existence, for it is by far the earliest of vernacular annals ; and the first entry in the *Chronicle* which tells a story, the famous account of the bloody feud between Cynewulf and Cyneheard, is remarkable for its narrative power. There were also on the Continent chroniclers at work in Latin. It is to some extent a European phenomenon I am discussing : but Old English is the earliest of the European vernaculars to achieve literary expression, and the sense of time is wide-spread in both old English poetry and prose, personally expressed by many minds in their own mother-tongue.

The Anglo-Saxons had a marked leaning to an imaginative unworldliness. In the eighth century, a golden age of achievement in many fields, the brighter in its contrast with the benighted ignorance into which the Continent had fallen, Englishmen seem to have flocked

into monasteries. Many became missionaries and
martyrs in Europe, laying the corner-stone for the
development of medieval Europe. Comparatively few
of the ablest minds turned their attention to directing
affairs at home. The sense of the passage of time issued
in a desire not to redeem the time so much as to escape
from time.

The centuries immediately following are less noticeably concerned with the passage of time, but in the major
authors, Chaucer, Langland, Malory, there is a sense of
the past rather similar to that of the Anglo-Saxons.
In Chaucer's *Troilus and Criseyde*, and in *The Man of
Law's Tale*, there is an attempt at secular history, a
genuine attempt to guess at the conditions of past life.
It does not extend very far, for there was not the material
available, but the attempt shows Chaucer's insight as
superior to all other contemporaries. Froissart, the
Belgian chronicler, for example, who thought and
wrote in French, has curiously little sense of the passage of time. He is essentially a diarist, making note
of splendid or interesting things he wants to tell people
about. Langland looks back to the Incarnation, and
we are reminded here of the constant interest in the past
exerted by the Bible. The unlettered contemporaries
of Chaucer and Langland, like those of Shakespeare,
were annually enacting, in the Miracle Plays, the whole
cycle of the earth's history, from the creation of Adam
and Eve to the Day of Judgment. Malory represents
another trend of thought, ' primitivism ', the praise of
the ' good old days '. The English were remarked in
the medieval centuries, twelfth to early seventeenth,

for the seriousness with which they believed that King Arthur was the last of the great kings of Britain; that he had died in the sixth century A.D.; and that he would, or might, come again. Malory, writing about the middle of the fifteenth century, looks back to the Arthurian Age of Chivalry with a profound regret which is unaffected by the record he gives of the treachery and failure which led to the final downfall of the Round Table.

The tendency in these later treatments of the past coincides with, or results from, other causes that were making men feel that the earth was, if a vale of tears, at least not a vale they wished particularly to hurry through. More value being attached to some period of the world's history, more value was attached to the world. The former contempt for the world was giving place to a feeling that it was legitimate to enjoy the world.

It is possible that the emphasis in medieval English stories on action and event, the impatience with reflection which is recognisable in English stories as contrasted with French, is not only a consequence of a more childish taste, but is also a product of a stronger interest in sheer event, a kind of historical passion for something to happen. This feeling for sheer narrative interest is not limited to the medieval English. Boccaccio has it *in excelsis;* Chaucer has it, but can and does sacrifice it to other interests. Nevertheless it seems more typical of the English than of the French or the Italians. It can be seen most clearly in Elizabethan drama, when we compare that with Greek drama, or

the Noh. Elizabethan and Jacobean drama is notable
for the large number of history plays. Does any other
body of drama contain so large a proportion? And the
history is serious history, the treatment usually of a
period of time, not simply the dramatisation of a striking
episode. Except for *Othello* even Shakespeare's major
tragedies are historical plays. Even when the play was
not historical, dramatists liked to treat a period of time,
sometimes as much as twenty years. This is the more
remarkable, because the whole pressure of critical
thought as expressed by Sir Philip Sidney, Ben Jonson
and others, condemned such extension in time. The
essential nature of Elizabethan drama, following the
medieval drama, is narrative and descriptive, concerned
continually with the flux of time. Like the Christianity which underlies it, Elizabethan drama is historical
and materialistic. Elizabethan drama does not grasp
at the timeless. It is peculiarly immersed in the con-
tingent and accidental, in the before and after.

It would be well, all the same, not to exaggerate this
quality in Elizabethan and Jacobean drama. There is
a strong sense of chronological development of *event*,
of one thing leading to another, but there is not much
sense of the chronological development of *character*,
except a little in Shakespeare. The only characters
of Shakespeare who really *develop* are the heroes of his
principal tragedies: Macbeth is the most striking example, Othello the least, Hamlet, the most uncertain.
Except with Hamlet, (and there much less than un-
historically-minded critics have realised) Shakespeare
has little interest in the personal motives which lead a

man to do a thing : he is much more interested in the
doing. It is usually profitless to speculate on the
motives of a Shakespearean character. Shakespeare,
naturally, knew that a man has them, but he treats them
casually. Iago, for example, on the occasions when the
dramatist feels he needs some motive for his malignity,
is casually supplied with several. They are enough to
quieten the mind of the audience, as they separately
occur. The centre of interest is not *why* Iago does such,
but the doing of it to Othello. Similarly it is pointless
to speculate on Lear's motives in dividing the kingdom.
He does it : that is enough ; and in this case it was, from
Shakespeare's point of view, historically well-attested,
well known to his audience, and therefore the less
provocative of interest. Our modern obsession with
motive is a product of late nineteenth-century developments.

The interest in plot, action, event, in English literature
from medieval times onward is, however, very strong,
contrasting very much with the typical literature of
Japan, and even, it would seem, with that of the rest
of Europe. In the seventeenth and eighteenth centuries
plot, action, and event abandoned the stage, and with
them went most of the literary interest of the drama.
Since the Restoration the English drama has rarely, with
the possible exception of Shaw, been at the growing-
point of the age. The interest in plot, in an interrelated
series of events, turned from the stage and, if such a
violent figure of speech may be permitted, seized the
long prose romance, compressed it, and turned it into
the novel. It is by the interrelated series of events and

by the interrelation of characters with those events that
we recognise the novel. These qualities the long prose
romance held in diffuse suspension. They were cryst-
allised out in the middle of the eighteenth century in
England. The novel has altered a good deal since then,
especially in other countries, but its characteristic
modern form, whatever its variations, starts from the
time when Henry Fielding and Samuel Richardson with
their very different attitudes and abilities, precipitated
their strong sense of time and character in a clear and
relatively concise prose fiction of, in Mr. Forster's useful
phrase, ' a certain length '. Of the convention of
character I shall say more later. The nature of plot,
that series of related events in time, is very clearly shown
in one of the earliest novels, Fielding's *Tom Jones*.
Coleridge may have exaggerated when he called the
plot of *Tom Jones* one of the three best in the world,
but it is certainly very good. The elaborate intertwining
of the various threads, yet the impression of a completely
natural succession of events; the unexpected en-
counters; the near misses; the agreement of action
with character; all these keep our interest continually
on the alert, while in the last book there is a masterly
heightening of suspense and increase of speed, and the
novel finishes with tremendous dash and interest.
Fielding spent years writing for the stage, and for all
its naturalism the firm outline of the plot is decidedly
stagey.

Perhaps from this melodramatic origin of the plot in
the English novel, perhaps from its inherent nature,
this kind of plot, and this sense of time, always places

great emphasis on the end. Even in the Middle Ages
the rhetoricians and the common proverbs of Western
Europe asserted that, in the words of Chaucer's Pandarus, ' the end is every tales strength '. This ' linear '
sense of time makes both beginning and end extremely
important. This emphasis on the end is comparable
only with our deaths, and perhaps not with them; our
ordinary experience of life sees very few clear-cut
endings. Greek literature does not seem to have set
much store by the ending—who remembers the end
of the *Iliad?* The Middle Ages, with their treatises on
The Four Last Things, on the Last Day, and (notwith-
standing Boethius's warning) with their incapacity for
envisaging eternity as anything but time-going-on-for-
ever, saw the establishment of the convention of the
ending, a necessary part of the sense of the passage of
time. The feeling for the ending seems particularly
strong in English literature : contrast here the nineteenth-century Russian novel with the English.

The novel was dominated by the plot throughout the
rest of the eighteenth and the nineteenth century. The
plot was necessary to the evolution of the novel, but it
often conflicted with other elements in it, especially the
treatment of character. Some novelists always found
their real interests inadequately buttressed by the scaffolding. Scott is the obvious example, with his difficulties of constructing an ' artificial and combined nar-
ration ' which he confesses to in the Introduction to
The Fortunes of Nigel. Dickens's varying and increasingly elaborate and successful treatment of the plot is
worth a study in itself ; and in Dickens, too, the con-

nexion between stage and novel in plot is obviously very
close.　In general, the domination of the ending became
so great that one may say that every nineteenth-century
novel, in order to achieve an ending sufficiently strong,
was forced to finish with either a wedding or a funeral.
In *The Mill on the Floss*, where neither is appropriate,
George Eliot was forced by social convention to turn
her notes to tragic, with the result that the ending
though effective in a melodramatic way has generally
and rightly been considered unsatisfactory in tone
compared with the earlier part of the novel.　Hardy's
Jude the obscure suffers in a similar way.

There was also in the nineteenth century a more profound development of the sense of time, representing
a real development of the imaginative power, and also,
there being no gain without loss, a real limitation of
the imagination, too.　The new stores of knowledge
amassed in the eighteenth century, the better command
over the materials of civilisation which improved travel
and the circumstances of learning, all made it possible
to recognise more easily the ' pastness of the past '.
The poetry of the eighteenth century is in its feelings
for the sombre and ruinous surprisingly close to some
of the moods of Old English poetry.　But up to the
end of the eighteenth century men saw time as a series
of successive points.　' There are in our existence '
says Wordsworth, ' *spots* of time '.　In the nineteenth
century men increasingly saw time as flow.　It is the
change from the conception of a mechanical universe
to an organic universe, a change still taking place in
our imaginations.　It is very characteristic that the

major scientific discovery of the nineteenth century, the Theory of Evolution, was, as Collingwood pointed out, an historical concept. It did not depend so much on new facts as on a new presupposition about the nature of the universe. The different presupposition about the nature of the universe in the nineteenth century appears in all sorts of ways. To take a purely literary example : Johnson's criticism of Shakespeare is often not understood because it is not realised that Johnson had no concept of chronological and hence artistic development in a writer's work. When criticising Shakespeare's tragedy in general terms he had *Titus Andronicus* and *Romeo and Juliet* equally in mind with *King Lear*. Small wonder that he said that Shakespeare's tragic style is often turgid. Immature works were judged on the same level as mature works. It was the great achievement of nineteenth-century European literary scholarship to establish the chronology of Shakespeare's works. We take it for granted, but it involved a remarkable development of the imagination, and a great step forward in understanding. The absence of this understanding in the eighteenth century is not due to Johnson's personal stupidity : the concept of development in time, the concept of immaturity and maturity and decay, is one that has been hard-earned by the thought of all kinds of dissimilar thinkers. It is one of the conventions that even now has to be consciously learned, and is only the property of the well-educated. Another example which illustrates the gap between Johnson and us is Johnson's view of language. For Johnson the English language could be, and indeed recently had been, refined

and polished.   It is as if language were a block of marble.
In early days it has rude strength and simple outlines.
Later it is worked upon, including the ' polishing ',
until it reaches a static perfection, called correctness.
The aim then was to preserve this correctness against
the decay of time, as a statue must be protected against
weathering.   Such was the aim of Johnson's *Dictionary*.
By the time he had finished his *Dictionary* Johnson
knew that to attempt to fix the language in one form
was ' as much an undertaking of pride as to lash the
wind ', but he never reached a concept of language as
organic growth.   That was reserved for the later
grammarians—not English, as it happens, but German
—with their ' roots ' of words, and ' strong ' and ' weak '
verbs, and their genealogical ' trees ' showing the relations of languages to each other.   This convention is
still strong today ; it may well be a truer representation
of the nature of language than the old static one, since
it recognises one of the cardinal facts of language, as
of life ;   continuous change.   But in other ways it
seriously misrepresents the nature of language.   We
can now see that there is a gap between even the more
recent convention and reality.

Valuable as our increased sense of the passage of time,
of the pastness of the past may be, it is well to notice
also that it has some disadvantages as well as advantages.
If it often adds to our sympathetic understanding of
men in the past, it is also liable to make us feel cut off
from them in a way that earlier men did not feel about
their predecessors.   When the medieval and renaissance
painters portrayed Christ or Ulysses wearing the every-

day dress of the painter's own time : when the actors in the Miracle Plays did the same ; when Chaucer thought of Troy in the physical terms of fourteenth-century London ; they were of course making historical errors, but they had a sense, often a true sense, of imaginative communion with the past that the very exactness of modern knowledge may deprive us of. It is a disadvantage to us, in some ways, that we cannot imagine Christ in shabby trousers and a jacket. It is interesting, and characteristic, that there has been no attempt in England to re-state ancient and mythical stories in modern terms as there very notably has been in contemporary French literature by such writers as Sartre and Anouilh.

In the twentieth century there has been an increasing preoccupation with the sense of time. The experiments in ' the stream of consciousness ' by Virginia Woolf and James Joyce are an attempt to render a more subjective impression of time than has usually been done. Grahame Greene has said that to render the passage of time is one of the greatest challenges to the novelist's technique. D. H. Lawrence in *The Rainbow* and *Women in Love* made an attempt to escape from the usual dominance of the succession of events in time as the explanation of character. We hardly know the Ursula of the second book better for knowing her background and parentage. In trying to escape from the old ' stable ego of character ' in these books, as Lawrence expressed it in a letter to Garnett, he was also trying to escape from the flux of time. Yet *The Rainbow* in its conception and in the first half at least is a marvellously rich evocation of the effects of the passage of time. Lawrence's previous book *Sons and Lovers* is as much under the dominance of the sense of time—though not of plot—as any nineteenth-century novel; and Lawrence's last novel is in many respects a return to conventional methods of story-telling. Mr. Eliot has similarly made an attempt to find ' the intersection of the timeless in time ', and so to extend our imaginative grasp of reality, but he has necessarily chosen, writing in the tradition he does, to approach the ' timeless ' rather as the Anglo-Saxons did, through history. History, personal and general, is the fugal *motif* of *Four Quartets*.

It would be possible to trace the concern with time, indeed the obsession with time, through many areas of English and Western civilisation, which contrasts in this respect so strongly with the older Eastern civilisations. But the concern with time seems especially a characteristic of English literature, even though not limited to it. For example, what seems a little surprising at first to an Englishman in Proust's great novel is the faintness of its sense of the passing of time. The past is vividly evoked into a kind of secondary present ; and as the very title shows, it is not the pastness but the ' lostness ' of time that is important ; *A la Recherche du Temps Perdu*. What is lost may be found. An English writer would be very unlikely to think so. And the title of the English version of Proust's work, brilliant translation as it is, gives a characteristically English slant of thought in Shakespeare's words, *Remembrance of Things Past*.

Very much more could be said, more profoundly I have no doubt, about this deep preoccupation with time. It affects, as it derives from, our religious concepts, it can be seen in our philosophy, science, social, political, even economic arrangements, as well as our literature. Wage-policies are shaped by it, as well as the *Four Quartets*. And it is a convention, a way of approaching reality, which by no means all races and cultures share. Every Westerner coming to Japan notices at its most superficial the different valuation put upon time. When he reads a Japanese novel he notices the preference for certain kinds of meditative and descriptive writing, a *dwelling* on things, a lack of plot and action. These are not merely superficial differences, they reflect a different *Weltanschaung*, not lightly to be judged either better or worse than another, and demanding above all to be understood.

VI

The Love-story

I have occasionally spoken of ' plot ' and ' story ' in similar terms, though they are not quite the same thing. A plot is a scheme of interrelated events. A story is that, but it is also likely to be more. A story is not a simple linking of ' and thens ', drawing us along by the exercise of our idle curiosity, as Mr. Forster would have it, though it is this, too. A plot is an abstraction ; a story is a plot in action, and may have a number of other qualities and functions, according to the story-teller's will. A story need not even be fiction.

Its chief literary characteristic is movement, and in fiction it usually needs some kind of a plot to hold it together, to act as its bony skeleton, as its scaffolding. According to the writer's taste and ability, plot and story are closely or loosely associated. In the best novelists the story is greater than the plot, but the story is not in conflict with the plot. In lesser writers or writers of less artistic interest and ability, there often is a conflict between story and plot. In this section, I shall speak of the story, in which I include the idea of plot, but may also include other elements.

All stories are based on Quests or Conflicts or both. There are traces of stories of both in Old English literature, especially in prose; but partly because almost all genuinely secular and popular Old English literature has been lost, and partly because of the inveterately otherworldly, elegiac and meditative temper of the best Anglo-Saxon minds of which there is any record, it is difficult to generalise about stories in Old English literature.

In the Middle Ages proper, especially in the fourteenth century, there is a great burst of story-telling, of which the best examples are in the work of Chaucer and Gower. It is a European movement: the roots are in classical antiquity and in ancient and modern folk-tales widespread through Europe, and there is a wonderful variety of subject-matter: but the dominant type of story is the love-story. However often we remind ourselves of the historical nature of the convention of love we find it hard, at least in the West, to remember how artificial a convention it is.

The convention of love in Western European literature from about the eleventh century to the twentieth, is a very nice example of what is meant by convention, and how it operates. The convention itself is local and artificial, yet it is based on the most natural and widespread of human experiences, that of the biological attraction between the sexes. There is plenty of writing in all literature upon the universally interesting subject of sexual attraction. But in Provence in the eleventh century, as probably most of the readers of this essay already know, there arose, under various social, economic, religious and literary pressures, a special formulation and expression of this universal interest, which spread so as to dominate the secular literary thought of medieval Europe. This domination has extended in various ways ever since, until now, its literary descendant an integral part of the triumphant American film industry, the influence of this half-serious, half-literary, wholly aristocratic medieval convention has spread throughout much of the earth. We have here, too, an excellent illustration of how a convention may change and change again, taking differing forms in different countries, and yet maintain, through its continuity, a sense of identity.

The most notable characteristics of the convention in its earlier form were, first that in a feudal, male-dominated society, it asserted the superiority of the woman over the man who loved her; and second, it asserted that to love the lady made the lover virtuous. (Hence the medieval name, *fine amour*, which is better than the modern term *courtly love*.) There seems nothing

inherent in the mere physical attraction between the
sexes to account for these elements of superiority and
refinement which were thought to accompany true love.
This brings us to the next point, that although there is
obviously a powerful working of physical desire in the
love-convention, it is no more than the basis of the
convention. In earlier times, and perhaps not so long
ago either, it was usual enough for a man expressing
the purest and most passionate devotion to his lady, to
have also his bastards. Another aspect of this same
matter was that especially in French literature, both
the lover and the lady might each be married to someone else. In English literature, however, this adulterous
situation rarely arises. Another characteristic of this
kind of love is that it is essentially adolescent; by
which I mean that it is especially the sort of passion that
is liable to be felt in late adolescence when physical
desire is at its hottest, acquaintance with the world at
its freshest, opinions and ideas least well based and most
absolute. This is the most vivid time of life, and a
time when new directions are taken which will be very
hard to change in later years. It is a very important
time of life. And yet one may feel that the importance
attributed to it in Western literature to the exclusion of
emotions felt at other times of life has been somewhat
excessive.

There are some further characteristics which deserve
notice. Although the lady (in the twentieth century she
becomes the girl) is the point to which all the action
draws, and whose superiority is agreed, she is, especially
in the earlier period, as much a symbol as a person. The

action was seen from the point of view of the lover, and the lady was a passive prize. It was still a man's world. Then again, it was essentially a story of difficulty and postponed achievement. ' The course of true love never did run smooth.' The difficulties were either external, and hostile circumstances kept the lover from his lady; or internal, where the lady herself was reluctant. Usually difficulties were both external and internal. The quality of love was static. The lover hardly came to know his lady better : the relationship did not develop—how could it, since the essence of the story was to keep the two apart until the last moment?

Although I have described, as far as possible, what is generally true of European *fine amour*, the English pattern is fairly distinctive within this larger form. One of the most marked differences, and a characteristic and important one, is that *fine amour* in English literature is in the rarest cases adulterous. Chaucer's *Troilus* may be a case of adulterous love, but if so it may well be, as I have argued elsewhere, a special case. The chief story of adulterous love in English is Malory's account in the *Morte d'Arthur* of Launcelot's disastrous love for Guinevere, which is based on a French source. It is characteristic that Malory attributes the tragic fall of the Round Table largely to this adulterous *amour*. It is also characteristic that the French story of Tristram's love for Yseult, wife of King Mark of Cornwall (which is also treated in the *Morte d'Arthur*) was never very popular in England, where Tristram's chief reputation was as a hunter.

In England therefore, very distinctively, *fine amour*

was treated from earliest times as the romantic love which came to its natural fruition in marriage. It is not until D. H. Lawrence that the central love-affair in a story came to be treated independently of marriage.

Lawrence's ideas on love, marriage and sex are not his alone. It is not difficult to find something similar to them in writers otherwise so dissimilar as Mr. Forster, and the almost forgotten best-seller Elinor Glyn. But the development of the modern convention of love in English literature is almost certainly largely due to the power with which Lawrence treats a theme which is peculiarly his. The lack of emphasis on sex, not very remarkable from Chaucer to Fielding, developed in the nineteenth century novel to an absurd omission, so that, as Thackeray complained, adult treatment of the full relationship between the sexes became impossible. Lawrence put the sex back into love, so to speak, and some might argue that in Lawrence there is too much sex and too little love. But Lawrence also emphasised perhaps more vigorously than anyone else, that love was for marriage, and marriage was for ever. It is hardly necessary to point out here the inconsistency that many of the love-relationships in Lawrence's work, like that in his own life, began with adultery. It is a curious inconsistency, characteristic of Lawrence, and characteristic perhaps of that type of English inconsistency which so easily appears to foreigners as hypocrisy. It is not hypocrisy since there is no attempt to conceal the inconsistency, but it may be self-deception, and it is certainly, from a logical point of view, a muddle.

The love-story in English also blends in a curious

way with humour and helps to produce the complex of the English sense of humour. The most important example is Shakespeare. The humour of the love-story is quite different from humour about sex. For various reasons, sex is good for a joke practically everywhere in the world. Jokes about sex may or may not appear in love-comedy : they are not essential to it. When Shakespeare began to write comedies he took as his main thread of narrative the medieval love-romance, as mediated through various sixteenth-century writers. Now one of the things the medieval love-story certainly was *not*, was comic.   Such exalted and strained emotions, if treated in conjunction with a humorous theme, could easily enough come to seem absurd. But from the necessities of entertainment Shakespeare felt bound to include in the early *Two Gentlemen of Verona* both a medieval love-story, and also ordinary knock-about comic turns—the cunning and stupid clown, whose dog urinates embarassingly, the witty, logic-chopping page. And as Professor Charlton pointed out long ago, the down-to-earth, coarse humour of the clown makes the high-flown sentiment of the love-story appear rather silly. The love-story Shakespeare chose is more silly than Chaucer's *Knight's Tale*, but the effect of the combination of the two elements in *The Two Gentlemen* is as if Chaucer had used *The Miller's Tale* as a sub-plot in the telling of *The Knight's Tale*. The development of Shakespearian comedy is essentially Shakespeare's progress in his ability to combine a love-story with humour. In *A Midsummer Night's Dream* the love-story is much the same as in *The Two Gentlemen*

with a similar episode of an attempted change of partners
even more central to the action.   But the story about
the lovers is protected from the charge of absurdity by
making the lovers the victims of the misapplied magic
charm.   The absurdities of love are thus gently mocked
in them, without the characters in their real selves suffering.   That the lovers themselves are gently mocked
shows a development in sophistication which also
protects them from too harsh a contact with the comedy
of Bottom.   In *Twelfth Night* and *As You Like It* there
is a further development.   The centre of interest is
shifted from the lover to the lady.   The lady is very
gently mocked, or rather, gently mocks herself for the
absurdities of love.   She also dominates the action—an
important change from the passivity of her role in
medieval romance.*   And above all she dominates the
tone of the plays, with her flashing wit, her intelligence
and her tenderness.   Of these perhaps the least recognised and most important is her intelligence.   Viola
and Rosalind especially, but the women in general, far
outshine all the men in their plays by the quality of
their minds, and even a Sir Toby Belch is thoroughly
controlled by a subsidiary heroine, Olivia, and set down

---

* The reason for the heroine's domination lies partly in the me-
chanics of the stage.   In medieval romance (like *The Knight's Tale*)
the main body of the story is taken up by the hero's activity, of which
some at least must be deeds of bravery and violence.   Shakespeare
must have rightly felt that the stage cannot well represent jousts, or
adventures—even Orlando's wrestling-match is off stage.   And so
the hero tends to be 'banished' to his activities; or is given a role
with little action.   In either case he attracts less interest.

by Maria the lady-in-waiting. When these brilliant
qualities are accompanied by a little physical weakness
of a kind sufficiently flattering to the male audience and
yet gladly enough accepted by women, the combination
is of irrestible charm. It is in the person of the heroine
that Shakespeare subsumes and adapts even the coarsest
comedy. The result of this blend of such delightful
heroines, a fortunate love-affair, and different kinds of
humour is that peculiar sunniness and sweetness of
disposition which is the final impression of Shakespearean comedy. The dominance of the heroine gives special
scope for the unique nobility and charity of Shakespeare's imagination.

The supremacy of the heroine is inherent in the love-
story. Even in Chaucer the hero tends to be a paler
character than the heroine. English literature is poor
in interesting young men. It may be that a young
woman is inherently a more poetic personage than a
young man, just as an old man is inherently more poetic
than an old woman, though the French, with their
Julien Sorel and their Athalie, the Germans with
Werther, might seem to deny this. There are a few young
heroes in English literature: Romeo, perhaps; Tom
Jones; Stephen Dedalus; possibly Lucky Jim (though
we are too close to judge him very certainly): the
number is small, at all events, compared with the array
of heroines of all kinds, and with the number of great
characters who are middle-aged and elderly men. The
young heroine and the love-story dominate non-tragic
fiction. Although this is a severe limitation, non-tragic
fiction in English has benefitted by the domination of

the love-story and its heroine in maintaining something of the sweetness and sunniness of Shakespearean comedy. The corollary of this is that writers have usually felt the need to escape from the love-story when they wish to reflect the darker, more severe, or more exalted parts of life. Hamlet's rejection of Ophelia is typical of all the more powerful or severe writing in English literature. There are remarkably few love-tragedies apart from Chaucer's *Troilus and Criseyde*, and Shakespeare's *Antony and Cleopatra*, and the latter is anyway not the usual kind of love-story. So that for all the importance of love and the young heroine in English literature, they are relegated to the background when most *really* important matters are being discussed. There is no English equivalent to Dante's Beatrice.

VII

Character

An essential part of the interest in the story is the interest in a particular convention of human character which is very strong in English literature, even though also found elsewhere. At its simplest the convention is that of the ' stable ego ' which Lawrence in *The Rainbow* and *Women in Love* attempted to get away from. Lawrence was particularly trying to get below the accretions of what he called the personality, and would have done better to call the character—that part of us which is more obviously the product of environmental conditioning ; he wished to get below this to the naked potentiality, the true *individual*. He gave a new sense of depth to the portrayal of men and women in literature, but he did not succeed in giving a very clear sense of the force and uniqueness of the bare individual.   The nearer he comes to the ' individual ' (and he never comes very near) the less individual the individual seems, the more he or she is a generalisation of Lawrence's current theory of the nature of human kind.   Skrebensky is the best example.   Lawrence failed to realise that the individual can only be the individual when in contact with the general :   the individual *per se* and the general *per se* are abstractions, like form and content in poetry :   they do not exist separately.

Lawrence's objection to the old presentation of character was presumably that it did not allow for the variability, the flux of identity, the ragged edges, we are all conscious of, or should be conscious of, in our own characters and in those of the people we know.   English literature tends to portray people with a number of fixed traits, and to rely especially on a visual presentation of character.   As Taine long ago pointed out, there is usually in English literature greater interest in moral questions and less interest in personal psychology. Lawrence himself, in his last book, *Lady Chatterley's Lover*, reverted to this external, static presentation of character, where the movements of the individual mind are less regarded than the moral implications of the various actions.   Lawrence's attempt to get away from the usual presentation of character in English literature represents a general trend of his time, shared by such unlikely bedfellows as Virginia Woolf and James Joyce. But great as Lawrence's and Joyce's and Mrs. Woolf's achievements are, they all seem to represent dead-ends of exploration. The general current seems to have re-asserted itself in the old channel in the most recent novels: we are back with the old driving narrative and the solid character. The contrast between English and French achievements may make the point clearer. The first two novels of Francoise Sagan, *Bonjour Tristesse* and *Un Certain Sourire* have been rightly praised for their psychological insight. They have little narrative interest, no outstanding events. Their charm and their power rests in the capacity to perceive with extraordinary clarity, and convey in the most delicate strokes, the feelings of a young girl in a certain situation. These novels are in a clear line of development from such short psychological novels (usually in fact autobio-graphical) as *Dominique* and *Adolphe*, going back, no doubt, to *La Princesse de Clèves*. We are reminded that even in the Middle Ages the French romances con-tained much description of states of feeling which English translators and imitators nearly always cut out. They wished to get on with the action. So the short psychological novel on a single theme has never flourish-ed, has never even been practised, in England. The characteristic conventions of time-plot and character have never favoured it.

The first unequivocally clear example of the English convention of character occurs in the series of portraits in Chaucer's *General Prologue to the Canterbury Tales*. The ' portrait ' was not invented by Chaucer. There is a series of portraits at the beginning of Benoît de Ste-Maure's huge poem on the fall of Troy, *Le Roman de Troie*, written in the third quarter of the twelfth century ; one of a group of French poems associated with the court of the Angevin and the English King Henry II. Probably Chaucer took the hint for his own series of portraits from Benoît. But the portrait itself is a favourite device of a number of especially northern medieval writers and its technique was discussed in the Arts of Rhetoric which formed the taste and technique of so many medieval writers, including Chaucer. Interest in the literary portrait itself goes back to the historical writing of late Greek and Roman literature, particularly of the second and fourth centuries. But its real development comes first in the French and Latin writers of the European twelfth century, and then, even more strongly, in late medieval English writing, especially, as I have said, in Chaucer. He takes and intensifies a common European trait, of which the first suggestion is found in late classical antiquity. The Anglo-Saxons seem not to have been interested in character—the dreaminess, the unworldliness, the taste for symbolic generality, which are so typical of the Anglo-Saxon mind, gave little basis for specific portraiture.

Chaucer's characters in *The General Prologue* are so vivid just because of the specific detail, especially the concrete detail of dress, with which they are described. But this is only successful because the detail, precise and individual as it is, has also symbolic or representative quality : we guess the person's inner character by his outward appearance. Chaucer was helped here by the social conventions of his day, according to which different classes and occupations dressed differently from each other. There were Sumptuary Laws to enforce these differences, and particularly to stop the lower classes aping the dress of their betters. Chaucer's Guildsmen, for example, are breaking the sumptuary law in having silver rather than brass handles to their knives. This detail is a good example of how Chaucer conveys social and moral significances through what at first sight seems the description of arbitrary or merely decorative outward appearances.

What is notable in Chaucer's portraits in general (Criseyde is an exception) is the lack of psychological interest, and the deep concern with social and moral 'placing' of a character. Elizabethan and Jacobean writers show much the same concern in outwardly presented characters. The seventeenth century both reflects the interest in character and advances the treatment of it with the great outburst of the 'character writers', of whom Earle is the best, but of which there are many minor practitioners. Again their descriptions are static, but they explore more fully the maze of individual character, they set up a wider range of types, they encourage that taste for the odd and eccentric character, which is found so frequently in the English novel; they helped to make, indeed, the English novel possible.

It would take too long to follow these suggestions through the wonderfully rich field of the English novel, from Parson Adams and Tom Jones onwards. It must be enough to suggest that this type of character-convention is both the strength and weakness of the English novel. It is a strength because it gives a strong sense of actuality to the novel ; we feel we really meet people, and really *see* the people whom we meet, in a novel. The convention administers to our lust for actuality, which since Chaucer, at least, has been typical of the English imagination. We can enjoy the spectacle of life in them. Furthermore, because the characters seem real, we can consider in and through them all sorts of moral and social arrangements. The weakness of this convention of character is that it makes it difficult to convey the inwardness of people, delicate nuances of feeling, fine distinctions of thought.

VIII

Class-distinctions

One of the important aspects of a character is his or her social class. Placing in social class, and relation to other persons in the same and other social classes are rarely left unsuggested in English literature. This is a subject of some complexity, both in literature and life, and a thorough study of the treatment of questions of class in English literature would be of great interest. Here I can only make some brief comments and suggestions to open the subject for further consideration. And one may add that as with other conventions, it is the kind of subject on which foreign readers may be able, through their detachment, to treat from a fresh and stimulating point of view.

The briefest reflection will show that no large society has existed or can exist without class distinction. But there are many different bases, often within the same society, for class distinctions; blood, occupation, intelligence, education, physique, money, possessions, are the most obvious. The class system may be rigid or flexible; just or unjust to individual merit; much or little regarded; but it is always there.

From the point of view of literature we may ask, what class or classes produce literature; and given a work of literature, to what class or classes is it directed, and which class or classes enjoy it and are affected by it. We may also ask how far literature reflects the class system, what attitudes to class are possible or favoured in literature, and how important the class system is to literature. As so often with literary studies, and perfectly properly, such a study will inevitably spill over into a study of part of the society which the work of literature arises out of. Unless literature has to do with life it is not worth bothering with.

A deep interest in the spectacle of society is common in English literature, and everywhere there is recognition and acceptance of class differences. The feeling is not the same at all periods. The grouping or stratification within a society is not at every period based upon the same qualifications, nor viewed in the same light. In the earlier period, up to in some cases the eighteenth century, one can hardly call the phenomenon a stratification at all. The different classes are part of the great chain of being which the created universe composes. In the Middle Ages the universe was felt to be bound together by the chain of love, as may be read in Chaucer's prose translation of Boethius, and in his verse translation of the same passage in *Troilus and*

Criseyde. In Shakespeare's time the concept had hardened to the chain of ' degree ' or rank, as explained in Ulysses' great speech in *Troilus and Cressida :* untune that string (of degree) and we may expect chaos to come again.   In Shakespeare the difference between the older medieval concept and a more modern concept is clearest seen in the clash between Sir Toby Belch, retainer of Olivia in the old style, and Malvolio, retainer in the new style.   Sir Toby is a relative, Malvolio a servant.   Shakespeare seems to have preferred the old style, being in this, as in other matters, rather old-fashioned in his likings.

The emergence of an urban middle class chiefly concerned with trade, and the increasingly money-based nature of society in the eighteenth century, for the first time in England began to produce a class-structure similar to the kind that is familiar from some nineteenth-century theorists.   The earlier class-structure was very different in feeling, depending ultimately on a different world-view.   But the coherence even of the newer class-structure is well evidenced in D. H. Lawrence's greatest novel, *Sons and Lovers*.   Although it was written at the end of the nineteenth century, and although there is an intense consciousness of class differences, and an intimate recognition of the poverty and suffering of the working-class from which Lawrence sprang, there is no class-animosity.   The concept of class-warfare, even in the most terrible days of the nineteenth century, has never been very realistic in England.   There is a basic instinct for ' hanging together ' in English society, as George Orwell in particular has pointed out.   One of the reasons for this is that the class-system, although usually well defined, whatever its basis, has never been exclusive; and there has always been a strong attempt to associate privilege and prestige with power. In accordance with this, as a man's power has increased, either through function or possessions or position, so his rank in society has been improved. There has never been any numerous equivalent in England to the ' poor samurai '. In the fourteenth century the church was the chief way of advancing one's status in society: but Chaucer, son of a wine-merchant, and never rich, moved familiarly in the highest circles of the land, as did rich merchants, who were usually given some degree of nobility. The famous family of the De La Pole's, Earls of Suffolk finally, had their origin in a merchant of Hull. Even in the eighteenth century there is record of two footmen who were eventually knighted. There can be few noble families at the present day in England which have not received, usually through marriage, strong infusions of blood and treasure from rich commoners in the nineteenth century.

All this is reflected and accepted in literature. How frequently, for example, do heroes marry above them. The typical heroine of the love-story is superior to the hero not only mentally and morally, but often socially as well. Of course there are plenty of exceptions, but I am speaking here of the general trend—Emily of *The Knight's Tale*. Rosalind, Olivia (not Viola, though) Tom Jones's Sophia, (though Richardson preferred humbler heroines) and particularly the nineteenth-century novelists from Scott onwards. The same tendency in Lawrence, backed by his and his father's personal experiences, is especially strong, and it continues in the novels of the new kind of social realism which have followed Mr. Amis's *Lucky Jim*, one of whose themes is the climb up the ladder of social prestige by a hero who begins from the lower middle class.

Feeling about class is particularly interesting in these post-war novels. The writers seem especially self-conscious about class-differences, and this reflects a similar and, one hopes, a passing tendency in English society today. The reason for it is not far to seek. The social revolution of the first post-war Government, bringing about the ' Welfare State ', and the general acceptance of this revolution by subsequent conservative governments, have caused wide-spread changes in the class-system. The class system in post-war England is based rather more directly on money than it was before, and the distribution of money has been much changed. Consequently, many people find themselves in a class higher or lower than that which they were accustomed to: and are therefore more sensitive than in the past both to their own behaviour and to that of their neighbours', because it is less easy to take behaviour for granted.

The great importance of the changes in British social life since 1945 can hardly be too much emphasised in Japan, where, except for a tiny informed minority, most ideas about English life are based on a little knowledge of the nineteenth century dressed up in the short skirts of the 'twenties and 'thirties.

Concepts often lag behind events. We have still—both English and Japanese—mainly nineteenth-century ideas about class structure, and these are the product of an early stage of a special state of society—modern industrial mass society—which was emerging for the first time in the history of the world in the nineteenth century in England. This state of society did not exist before, so that the concepts for understanding it were not to hand; it has moreover continued to transform itself with astonishing and increasing rapidity ever since its emergence, so that it is especially difficult to keep new concepts up to date. New concepts are continually required and thus it is that nineteenth-century concepts of class are inadequate both for understanding the present day and for understanding earlier periods. Even the simple division of upper, middle and lower classes, rather characteristic of the eighteenth and nineteenth centuries, needs to be used with great care. It does not represent in any adequate way the structure of modern English society. Its apparent similarity to the medieval theoretical division of society into Knights, Clergy, Ploughmen, is as much misleading as helpful. It tells us little about the structure, theoretical or actual, of English society of the sixteenth and seventeenth centuries.

Probably no class structure is properly to be understood without consideration of something much deeper, the bonds of society. What makes men submit to each other? It may be mere physical fear. But except possibly in a police state, this is never likely to be the whole truth. A whole people cannot be entirely coerced. A

people must in some way worship the same gods as its
leaders worship, or as its leaders pretend to worship.
All men in a functioning society give at least part of
themselves in willing allegiance to some general governing ideas; an idea of the state, of the nature of man
and of his place in the universe, in a word to ideas of
duty or obligation which are absolute and which hold
the society together. This non-materialist loyalty,
this metaphysical compulsion, has been seen nowhere
more strongly in the last few years than in the true
devotees of Communism. Its source may vary from
mere gregariousness to religious faith, or to the secular
perversion of religious faith. But weak or strong, most
men in a society share it, and it is what keeps a society
going. Few men lose it, and when they do they become
singularly contemptible. Shakespeare has shown such
a one: his name is Parolles.

The bonds of society in England were those provided
by Christianity, but were different from those of even
closely similar Christian societies. Dominant in them
is the concept of Law, of law as emanating from God,
and to which human law should always attempt to
approximate. The classic statement of this doctrine
is Book I of Hooker's *Laws of Ecclesiastical Polity*, and
no one can fully understand, for example, what Shakespeare meant in his tragedies without knowing this
noble piece of writing, which sums up the English
view of centuries of medieval and classical thought.

Once again, my aim is to suggest a topic in relation
to literature, rather than to explore it, and the reference
to law raises another vast set of characteristic con-

ventions which must at least be mentioned. These are
the conventions of religion and morality.

IX

Religion and Morality

It is sometimes said that the English have no religion
but a double dose of morality. What is meant, presumably, is not that the English are more moral than
other people, but that they are more interested in morals
or are more moralistic, while they have little taste or
capacity for the transcendencies of religion. The
generalisation points in the right direction. The subject is too conplex for any generalisation to do more.

The first thing to say about religion in English literature, however, is simply that it exists. Nowadays we are
in the extraordinary position of having English scholars
of English literature apparently arguing that Shakespeare
was not a Christian. On all grounds both of internal
and external evidence, this is an absurdity. The absurdity is the basis of plenty of misunderstanding. My
later chapter on Shakespeare examines in detail the
implications of one part of Shakespeare's Christian
belief, the immortality of the soul, which will serve as
a good example of a religious convention of thought and
feeling. It is worth remembering that belief in the
immortality of the soul is an essential part of Christian
belief, though it may be variously interpreted, and this
particular concept is of great importance for the way it
modifies behaviour and attitudes, especially with regard
to death. The strength of the belief in immortality

strongly affects the pattern of feeling of two great fourteenth-century poems, *Troilus and Criseyde* and *Pearl*. In each it gives a special tenderness of feeling and a special toughness of thought, which are very unfamiliar today and which (leaving aside the truth or otherwise of the doctrine of immortality) it is well worth while for the twentieth century at least to recognise, if it cannot recover. The concept has helped to make man's feelings fuller and more tender, and at the same time less sentimental. This is especially the case in *Pearl* where the father's tender feeling for his dead two-year old daughter is developed in the most moving and convincing way. The combination in this poem of deep, tender and varied paternal feeling with energetic rational thought and highly elaborate style makes it as great as, perhaps greater than, anything Chaucer ever wrote.

So strong is the belief in immortality that we can move from the fourteenth century to the beginning of the nineteenth and find Keats and Shelley, who were not Christians, proclaiming their belief in immortality : and we can move from there to Mr. Forster, who is anti-Christian, remarking in the last sentence of *The Hill of Devi* of his dead friend, ' He has the rare quality of evoking himself, and I do not believe that he is here doing it for the last time.' This is typically vague, tentative and ambiguous, like all Mr. Forster's approaches to major questions of this kind. Taken in conjunction with his other beliefs, if it means what it seems to mean, it must be regarded as a quaint survival of a belief acquired from Christianity. On the other

hand it can be justified as showing that very sense of
mystery which helps to make him a great novelist.
However we regard it, there it is: and the presence of
such vague hints about immortality is one of the supports which helps to make *A Passage to India* the great
book it is. D. H. Lawrence is instructive too. He
seems to have had no belief in actual immortality,
but he is continually drawing on the wells of feeling
concealed in the word *eternity*. Younger modern
writers of any significance known to me do not however
reveal any belief or any interest in immortality. This
is an aspect of the modern ' decay of religious sensibility '. It is enough to say for the moment that the
belief in immortality, though not important in some
writers, is a constant in English literature, and inevitably has an effect on scales of values, even when not itself mentioned or consciously thought of.

One very important fruit of the religious imagination
in England has already been briefly mentioned—the
veneration for Law. The veneration for Law seems
very characteristically English, and is the more worth
pointing out since such a feeling would appear to be
quite absent in Japanese culture. I do not mean that
the modern Japanese people are less law-abiding than
the modern English. But there seems to be no concept—why should there be?—of law emanating from
God; and in consequence, there is not the special
feeling for man-made law that exists in England. In
England man-made law is held in respect because it
is the Law: but it is always liable to be compared with
an ideal of the Law which to some extent controls, or

tries to control, actual laws. In Japan it is very noticeable that the regard for the law is different. In high
and low affairs there are two processes : first, to discover what the law is ; secondly, to decide whether or
not to apply it. I venture this rather crude piece of
sociology not for its own sake, but to try to underline
my understanding of the place the law holds in the
English imagination. George Orwell has graphically
described this place in modern life in his brilliant if
occasionally exaggerated essay *England Your England*
(which should be set reading for every foreign reader
of English Literature). The feeling for law derives
largely from medieval European Christian thought which
came to emphasise in a thousand ways in literature and
otherwise the law and order of the created universe.
The whole universe obeyed the law ; only man had
disobeyed, though even he, by his own efforts and
with the help of Grace might turn his footsteps back
to old track of righteous obedience from which he had
strayed. In Elizabethan and especially Shakespearean
tragedy (and comedy too, for that matter) the setting is
a universe governed by God's law, where man has
disobeyed, but where he can, if he will, find redemption and salvation. This is the general convention—
an ordered universe. To the extent that modern science
presupposes an ordered universe it is still building on
this convention of Christian thought, even if in taking
over the convention it has quite properly for the purpose
in hand disregarded the religious and moral intuitions
that accompanied it, just as medieval Christianity built
on, and disregarded parts of, Greek, Latin and Arabic

scientific and religious thought in building up its own picture of an ordered universe. The way in which the universe is thought to be ordered varies in England in different centuries, but it is not until we come to the twentieth century that the tragedy of man can be conceived of as his presence in a morally unordered, a fundamentally arbitrary and purposeless universe. Up to the brink of the twentieth century even such a writer as Hardy (very nineteenth-century, for all his death in 1928) who is, or attempts to be, an atheist, has to invent a ' President of the Immortals ' to give full expression to his concept of tragedy at the end of *Tess of the D'Urbervilles*. Implicit in this hateful President is a universe not purposeless, unordered and indifferent, but one that is positively hostile, with its own dark order and purpose. English writers who lived much of their lives in the nineteenth century, in a powerful religious tradition, found it impossible, even though their minds rejected all kinds of religious faith, to empty their imaginations so easily. Mr. Forster and D. H. Lawrence are good examples. It is only really twentieth-century writers who have been able to empty their imaginations of religious faith, and even of them, members of the earlier generation, as for example Virginia Woolf, still seem often sensitive to the gap, as of the aching hole of a recently extracted tooth. It is only comparatively recently that writers seem to have had both the will and capacity to accept a complete lack of ultimate and hence religious significance in life, though these writers still show much, if satirical, interest in the moral qualities of people and in the morality of various social arrangements.

Religion in English writers seems to have issued most frequently into specifically moral channels.   How often does such a man as Fielding seem to be quite lacking in personal religious experience ; and yet he has a strong belief in Providence, a very strong moral sense (even though his heroes often break the laws of morality) and a tender compassion for his fellow creatures.   There are plenty of exceptions to this pattern of religious feeling in each century, and it barely emerges before the fifteenth or sixteenth centuries, but it is fairly constant after that time, for all the exceptions offered by a Herbert, a Law, a Blake, a Newman ; and it is the general trend I wish to suggest.   Shakespeare fits into this general pattern so well that some modern critics, as I have mentioned, actually question his religious conviction.   And to this pattern of feeling one might attribute the apparent weakness of the mystical tradition in England compared with some other European countries.

It may be that the insistence that religious devotion is a private matter, which is a firm modern English belief, is also a part of earlier religious feeling, and that a certain shyness about inner experience, or a reluctance to face inner experience is present in English literature. This may account for the absence of great English mystical writers (though there are some that are very good) and the enduring general distrust of ' enthusiasm ' in the older sense of that word.   Up to nearly the middle of the nineteenth century it was possible to praise a devout person, as I have seen written on a commemorative tablet of 1836, for being ' pious without enthusiasm '. It is instructive in this regard to compare the tone of

the *Ancrene Riwle* written about 1210, with the writings
of Bernard of Clairvaux on which it is largely based.
Bernard is powerful and passionate, straining upwards
all the time. The English is sincere and devout, but
far more earth-bound ; shrewd, practical, *homely;* and
humorous at times. Part VII of the *Riwle* is closely
translated from Bernard's Seventh Sermon in Lent.
The English author omits all Bernard's references to
mystical experience, and adds a number of concrete and
homely ideas and phrases. The tone of the English
as shown up by the contrast with the source strikes one
as typical of English feeling in any century. The desire
for private devotion comes out in unusual form in the
fifteenth and sixteenth centuries in Englishmen's passionate desire to have the Bible in their own tongue—
a privilege modern Englishmen take for granted and
ignore, but for which their forefathers were ready to
die.

There is also in English religion throughout the
centuries a vein of scepticism or mild irreligion, un-
accompanied by cynicism or (except in the bitter con-
troversies of the early sixteenth century) by really fierce
anti-clericalism and militant atheism. It would not
be impossible to attribute some of the author of *Beowulf's*
interest in pre-Christian heroes to the toleration arising
out of this state of mind, but to do so would be mere
guesswork, for the evidence from Old English times is
too incomplete, and the conditions of these times too
remote, for much to be said about them in this regard.
Chaucer as usual is the most obvious starting point, not
because he is at the beginning of a tradition, but because

he is the first great poet about whose times and works
we have sufficient information. There can be no doubt
that Chaucer was a devout Christian. His many
' books of legends of saints, and homilies, and morality,
and devotion ', beside the whole cast of his imagination,
bear witness to his faith and make it impossible to think
him insincere. But he, like most writers of his age,
and very noticeably his great contemporary Langland,
has little that is good to say of churchmen. Chaucer,
like Langland, could however create an ideal priest,
and his anti-clericalism is never directed against the
Church as a whole. (Even the more excessive Puritan
hostility against bishops and all they stood for in the
sixteenth and seventeenth centuries did not lead to
disbelief.) Beyond anti-clericalism, however, there is
a positive scepticism in many writers. This is partly
the scepticism of men, well educated in the arts and
sciences of their times, towards such priestly tricks as
practised on ignorant credulity, like the trade in spurious
relics with magical properties carried on by the Pardoner,
or the annual liquefaction of the Holy Blood, as practised
at Hales. This kind of scepticism came to a head in
the 16th century dissolution of the monasteries, when
the Commissioners actually investigated the Blood of
Hales. The scepticism of Chaucer can go deeper than
that, as when in *The Knight's Tale* he refuses to comment
on the destiny of souls. This scepticism is not the sign
of a profound unease, suppressed by the conscious mind,
or by that mysterious instrument of medieval oppression
known to some writers as the Church. It should not
be exaggerated into a nineteenth- or twentieth-century

expression of deep religious doubt. Rather it is a kind
of levity, a temporary release from the strain of considering serious matters seriously. Nevertheless, comparatively trivial as it is, it is there, and should be reckoned
with.

In the eighteenth century scepticism for the first
time in any large number of people becomes important.
There is a well-known passage by Bishop Butler in the
Advertisement to his *Analogy of Religion* (1736) where
he writes:

> It is come, I know not how, to be taken for granted by
> many persons that Christianity is not so much as a subject
> of enquiry; but that it is now at length discovered to be
> fictitious. And accordingly they treat it as if in the present
> age this were an agreed point among all people of dis-
> cernment; and nothing remained but to set it up as a
> principal subject of mirth and ridicule, as it were by way
> of reprisals for its having so long interrupted the pleasures
> of the world.

The ' reprisals ' are in themselves characteristic of
English scepticism, which from its traces in Chaucer
and its flowering in Gibbon, Hume and Bertrand
Russell, has often been graced with cheerfulness and
a good style. From the eighteenth century onwards
scepticism has been more and more important, and
has split away from faith as it had not in Chaucer.
And yet, so far, it has not been predominant in the
English imagination. Even writers like Hardy, and
Mr. Forster, as has been noted, seem to be bound to
invent (to put it at its lowest) some kind of supernatural
machinery in their novels, when they wish to release the

greatest possible amount of power.   It will be interesting to see if the most modern writers can maintain a large imaginative structure without recourse to hints of the supernatural.   The problem does not arise in short poems or stories.   It is only when the subject is great, and when a single work of literature attempts to render something suggesting a total picture of the world, that this particular problem arises.   A religious implication seems to have been successfully avoided by such great French writers as Stendhal and Proust.   There is no doubt that as Mr. Eliot notes, there is a genuine decay of religious sensibility in English writing today, and perhaps some great English writer will arise, or has already arisen, whose imagination will find no need to draw openly or covertly on religious thoughts, feelings, hints or guesses.   It will be an unusual phenomenon in a great English writer.

X

General Comments

It is tempting to venture some general comments on the character and temper of English literature, as it appears in the conventions I have described.   For a characterisation of English literature in full, a much lengthier study would of course be required.   And perhaps such a characterisation would be better performed by a foreigner than by a native.   Yet something may be said.

The first thing that strikes one is the capacity to maintain continuity within continual change.   The chief break appears between *Beowulf* and Chaucer, arising out of non-literary historical circumstances. When compared with this, other changes are far less violent. In particular there is no violent change between the Middle Ages and the Renascence, but only a slow process of development. It may well be, as Mr. C. S. Lewis has suggested in his *De Descriptione Temporum*, 1955, that the greatest change of all will prove to have occurred in the nineteenth century, between the Christian and post-Christian eras, arising out of what I describe in the last essay of this book as ' the crisis of expansion '. But so far the most representative writers of the modern period, though they explore new aspects of society, do so in very characteristically English ways. The view of character in English literature is at all periods a social and a moral one, rather than a psychological one. There is always a strong consciousness of the nature of time, an insistence on events, cause and effect. The place of women is always an important one, though not quite as important as it sometimes seems. There is little transcendental religious feeling, but a pervasive moral passion that usually depends for its sanction on a religion taken somewhat for granted. Side by side with religious feeling is an easy-going scepticism. It has occasionally been thought odd that such a pragmatical people, concerned so long with trade and industry, should produce such a body of great poetry. But the surprise merely depends on a nineteenth-century view of poetry as concerned with decorative beauty and not with real life. The poetry of the English is not, except in the nineteenth century, concerned especially with obviously beautiful objects : Chaucer and Shakespeare, Pope and Johnson, are concerned with society, Milton with man and God, Wordsworth with the mind : and modern English poetry is equally concerned with society and with the mind and heart of man in society.

THE HUMOUR
OF CHAUCER: THE ARTIST AS INSIDER

I

The Nature of Humour

Humour is not a convention itself, but it is governed by conventions of thought and feeling. Humour is awkward to write about, for serious discussion of it may seem an absurd contradiction in terms. But the criticism of tragedy is not expected to be tragic, and there is no need for the criticism of comedy to be comic. A greater difficulty is our lack of understanding of the bases of humour. We have to cut our way through such confusions as the idea that the most notable charac- teristic of the English sense of humour is its kindliness, and the idea that Chaucer is the very fount of what H. W. Garrod calls the 'loving-kindness of comedy'. The truth is that little humour is predominantly kind and all humour implies a limitation of sympathy that may amount to positive unkindness; while Chaucer is remarkable for the bland hostility of much of his humour.

It is necessary first to be clear about the nature of humour. It has no essential bond with smiling and laughter. One can be amused without either smiling or laughing, while on the other hand, smiling and laughing may indicate states of feeling other than amusement, and frequently do so in Japan.

Since humour is a personal reaction to the outside world it is convenient to distinguish the subjective and objective elements. The objective element is whatever in the outside world causes amusement to the observer. This objective element may be called the ' comic ', though it is also often called the absurd, the ridiculous, the funny, etc. The subjective element is the capacity in a human being to respond to the comic as comic; and this capacity to perceive the comic may be called the ' sense of humour '. The total humour-situation requires both subjective and objective elements to be present; there can be no humour if the observer is incapable of perception and response, or if there is nothing for him to respond to. The sense of humour and the comic are like the back and the front of the coin that is ' humour '.

Understanding of the nature of humour comes most easily from definition of the comic, which has been frequently done. It is generally agreed that the essence of the comic is the presence of incongruity or dispro-portion of some kind. This implies the presence of two contradictory aspects, which are however indis-solubly linked. Both the contradiction and the unity are vital. If the sense of unity were not present, the contradictions would simply fly apart. If unity is totally dominant, there is no sense of internal contradic-tion, that is, of incongruity or disproportion. Further, it is clear that the two elements which are in contradic-tion must be in some sort of balance. One may in fact be a good deal stronger than the other ; but it must not be so strong as to destroy the other. If the stronger destroys the weaker, the contradiction, and hence the incongruity, will cease to exist, and the comic is no longer comic. Nevertheless the opposing elements are not bound to be exactly equal.

The most obvious and simplest examples of the comic will illustrate these points. The old gentleman slipping on a banana-skin or chasing his hat provides an example of incongruity: the dignity of age contrasts with, is contradicted by, the indignity of his actions. If the undignified action is so complete as to wipe out our sense of the old gentleman's dignity, then the episode will seem not comic but pathetic or unfortunate. If he could retain his dignity, if there were no indignity to contradict it, there would also be nothing to amuse us.

But the opposing incongruities of the comic are only half the story, or less: the rest of the story is the observer's response to the comic. What it seems to happen in the observer is that he experiences a clash of feeling corresponding to and evoked by the incongruity of the comic. In the example of the old gentleman, whose dignity contrasts with his undignified antics, both inescapably part of him, the observer responds with respect for his dignity and disrespect for his indignity. Since both respect and disrespect are aroused by the same object, and are felt at the same time by the one observer, the two contradictory feelings are indissolubly united, just as the incongruous elements of the comic are indissolubly united. And just as the two clashing elements of the comic must be in some sort of equilibrium, so must the two clashing feelings in the observer be in some sort of equilibrium. If the observer sees the old gentleman slip on a banana-skin and hit his head very hard he is less likely to laugh: he may simply have one feeling of concern and anxiety, which is not offset by any contrasting feeling. Therefore he will not be amused.

For the sake of a clear illustration I have taken a situation of simple humour, and I have described the observer's feelings even more simply. Even in a situation like this it is unlikely that the observer's feelings would be simple respect and simple disrespect. He would be more likely to have what one may call a cluster of feelings: but they would resolve themselves into two groups which would conflict with each other. (It is probably the physiological tension caused by conflicting feelings which is sometimes relieved by laughter. Laughter is clearly associated with some kinds of emotional and hence physiological tension.)

The incongruity which constitutes the comic, and the corresponding emotional conflict arising from the perception of the comic, which is the sense of humour, may take a thousand forms. It seems likely that the nature of existence and the nature of man being what they are, there is nothing which may be perceived which is not potentially comic. There is always a possible clash between the different elements of existence. This is what validates Bergson's limited, though as far as it goes perfectly true definition of the comic, as the imposition of the mechanical upon the vital, of dead automatism upon living spontaneity. Bergson's definition gives just another example of the incongruous which is the comic.

If what I have said so far is true, though simplified, we may better understand two characteristics which are often attributed to the sense of humour. The one is the typically French view of Bergson that the sense of humour is concerned with social correction; and the other is the typically modern English view that the sense of humour in general, or at least the unique English sense of humour, is kindly. It will be noticed that these views are diametrically opposed. The view represented by Bergson derives from the classical one. Aristotle and Cicero, to quote representative classical thinkers, and Sidney, Hobbes, Hazlitt and George Eliot, representing earlier English thought on the subject, all emphasise the derisive, contemptuous quality of humour. The earliest example of the opinion that humour is kindly that I have noticed is the remark in *The School for Scandal*, Act II, Scene 2, that ' true wit is more nearly allied to good nature than your ladyship is aware of '. Very few of the great English humorists have been kindly—not Chaucer, Ben Jonson, Dryden, Pope, Swift, Thackeray, nor most of Dickens. There is much positive unkindness in all these authors. Of others the truth is that much of their humour is neither kind nor unkind, as Shakespeare, George Eliot, Hardy. Scott is perhaps the most kindly of the great humorists. The insistence on kindness is witness to the modern English idolatry of kindness (a different thing from love). When it comes to the test, however, though we like to be witty ourselves there are very few of us who care to be inadvertently the cause of wit in others. We do not like being laughed at, in however kindly a fashion. Yet other things being equal, we do not object to being spoken to, or treated with, kindness. We know in our hearts if not in our minds the divided, ambiguous nature of humour.

In our necessarily divided response to the comic in human nature there is very often both attraction, or at least sympathy, fellow-feeling; and repulsion. Both the old view of the hostility and contempt in humour, and the new view of kindliness and sympathy in humour, are true. The new, English view, sees an element in humour that is truly there, and this is a discovery, for the older critics, and the French, to go no further, never recognised the kindly and sympathetic element. But in emphasising kindliness the English over-emphasise sympathetic fellow-feeling, and disregard the element of hostility and contempt. In so doing they sentimentalize humour, and make it more of a puzzle than it really is. For there is no necessity for humour to be either kind or unkind. When we are concerned with the comic in human beings it is always likely that the incongruity will cause attraction and repulsion, since these are almost inevitable in any contact between one human being and another. But there is much that is comic that need not arouse this kind of personal feeling. There is a well-known story of a woman who when confronted with the American Revised Standard Version of the Bible said, 'The King James Version was good enough for Jesus and is good enough for me.' When I first heard this it seemed to me to be amusing.

The incongruity might be described as a chronological one: the idea of a first-century Jesus reading a seventeenth-century publication. There is nothing particularly sympathetic or hostile in that. Much humour is of this kind. But the joke illustrates another point of some importance. I should not expect the non-Western and non-Christian reader to feel more than the slightest flicker of amusement at this remark, partly because he would not have so clear a time-sense, but chiefly because he would have little or no potential feeling about the Bible or Christ. Beyond the elements of contradiction in unity we must also posit a capacity to arouse strong feeling in the material of the comic, and especially a capacity to arouse ambivalent feeling. This is why sex is a good subject for joking in all societies (at least, I have never known or read of a society in which sexual jokes were not made.) This is not a question of ' dirty jokes '. Perfectly proper sexual jokes may be made. Everybody feels strongly about sex. Sexual desire being what it is, it inevitably raises tensions in any civilised person, and the sense of humour can easily play upon those tensions. Because of the prepared ground it needs less effort to be funny about sex than about some more neutral thing. If we are to make a joke about something more neutral, we must build up the feelings in order to produce the tension.

By tension I do not mean strain. As I have said, there must always be some kind of equilibrium. Here physical metaphors fail; but we must imagine two forces opposed and in some kind of equilibrium, yet with one of the forces possibly stronger than the other. That is, humour may be predominantly hostile, but yet may be composed of a mixture of hostility and sympathy. The essence of the literary criticism of humour must be to attempt to understand what kind and intensity of feelings are in conflict. A joke demands as much analysis as a lyric. There is an infinite range of the emotional possibilities in humour, and it must be said that there has been very little critical thought devoted to them. The usual practice of literary critics, especially critics of Chaucer, is to assume that humour is either self-explanatory or beyond analysis, and to think that if one has said that such-and-such a remark is humorous, one has done all that is necessary. The aim of the present essay is to try to go further than has yet been directly attempted in the analysis of Chaucer's humour. I do not flatter myself that I shall get very far. The subject is very difficult, and there seem to be no masters to follow. My chief hope and chief excuse will be that the wreckage of my own attempt may serve to help other mariners avoid the rocks and fare further to better profit.

It will be simplest to work from the comic as it appears to us in Chaucer's work.

The chief comic subjects in Chaucer are, in the most general terms, himself; social class; literature and learning; women; ' hypocrisy '. There are also some additional minor topics, like sex, drink, manners of speech. The major subjects are however very large, and it is necessary to be more precise. Furthermore, I have used ' hypocrisy ', for want of a better word, in a rather special sense.

It is also worth briefly noting what does not provide the comic for Chaucer : religion ; professional occupations with the exception of the Merchant's and Lawyer's in the *General Prologue to the Canterbury Tales* (and in the latter case it is rather the Lawyer than the law) ; the knightly class is never found to be comic ; nor the labouring poor ; nor clothes ; nor nudity ; nor food ; nor physical elimination (contrast Pope and Swift) ; nor foreigners.

II

The Book of the Duchess

The major fourteenth-century English poets, Chaucer, Langland, Gower and the *Pearl*-poet, all introduce themselves into their own poetry. It was a convention of medieval European poetry. When a poet read his own poem to a familiar audience, to introduce himself dramatised the actual situation, gave a sense of verisimilitude, and provided an obvious point of departure for an exploration which was not primarily or directly concerned with the poet's personal thoughts and feelings. None of these other poets, however, introduces himself with the frequency and detail of Chaucer.

Chaucer's first appearance is in his first long poem *The Book of the Duchess*. The ' I ' of the poem is a *persona*, very lightly sketched in, based on the French convention of the unaccepted and sleepless lover. The poem is an elegy, and one would not expect to find humour in it. Nor is there. No person reading the poem with a mind uncorrupted by obsession with

Chaucer's humour could think it intentionally funny
at any point.   Where the poet mentions his own feelings
it is simply to say that they were very sad.   A reader
with inadequate control over his own risibility might
sometimes smile at the poem, finding it unintentionally
comic.   The poem is occasionally a little clumsy, its
frequent lists tend a little to naive exhibitionism, and
faults like these may amuse some, but amusement at
errors and inadequacies has obviously nothing to do
with Chaucer's humour.

III

The House of Fame

The next main poem was probably *The House of Fame*,
and Chaucer again introduces himself into the poem.
In Book I the ' I ' of the poem is the same simple
starting and recording device of the usual convention,
but in Book II Chaucer moulds the convention to his
own individuality in several ways.   The most obvious
is that he makes much more realistic the references to
himself, and to his daily, physical circumstances.   The
famous passage about his daily work, cooped up with
his accounts, and his reading in the evening, and his
ignorance of what goes on at his very doors (ll. 643–
60) is the nearest we ever come to straightforward auto-
biography in the whole of Chaucer's work.   He also
gives his own first name (l. 729).   And at the very
beginning of the Book (ll. 560–6) he makes a private
joke to his audience who must certainly have understood the veiled reference to real life.   The *persona* is

thus clearly established in realistic terms of the poet himself. It is highly likely for a number of reasons too lengthy to go into here, but generally accepted, that Chaucer first published his poems by reading them to a group of friends and intimates, or to the King's Court as a whole—the first group was anyway part of the second. So the audience knew the poet well, apart from his poetry. The audience knew him as an accomplished courtier; a trusted envoy on important diplomatic and financial missions; an important Port of London official; a reader of French, Latin and Italian poetry, of Latin philosophy, of Latin and French devotional works; an astronomer. In short, an ambassador, a high Government Civil Servant, a brilliantly learned man, a well-known poet. He presents himself in his poem, he presents, that is, his *persona*, as a dull overworked fellow, unlucky in love, solitary, ignorant (l. 867), fearful. The basis of the comic here is the incongruity between the real Chaucer and the *persona*. It is a good illustration of the nature of the comic. The real Chaucer and the *persona* are indissolubly associated because they are the same person : and they are also incongruous. It may be objected that since we do not know the real Chaucer ourselves we cannot possibly appreciate the clash of incongruities. It is obviously true that we lose something. We cannot appreciate the poem with the fresh sharpness of the audience for whom it was originally intended. But we do not lose all, for the equally obvious reason that the real Chaucer is represented by the whole poem. The clash between the real and the *persona* is conveyed by the relationship of the whole poem to the smaller figure of the *persona*.

One can only imagine the rich effect of that first reading, if Chaucer (as I for one find it hard to doubt) had any talent at all for reading. In the best comic acting, as opposed to tragic acting, we need to be conscious of the actor as well as of his impersonation—it is another version of the duality of the comic. Lamb is the earliest to notice this, when he writes ' On Some of the Old Actors ' about Jack Palmer :

> Jack had two voices—both plausible, hypocritical and insinuating ; but his secondary or supplemental voice still more decisively histrionic than his common one. It was reserved for the spectator ; and the dramatis personae were supposed to know nothing at all about it. The *lies* of young Wilding, and the *sentiments* in Joseph Surface, were thus marked out in a sort of italics to the audience. This secret correspondence with the company before the curtain (which is the bane and death of tragedy) has an extremely happy effect in some kinds of comedy, in the more highly artificial comedy of Congreve or of Sheridan especially, where the absolute sense of reality . . . is not required . . .

Some such ' double voice ' we may well imagine Chaucer using in a dramatic reading, suiting his actions to his words, like a well-educated gentleman such as the envoy in *The Squire's Tale* who spoke with manly voice:

> After the forme used in his langage,
> Withouten vice of silable or of lettre ;
> And, for his tale sholde seme the bettre,
> *Accordant to his wordes was his cheere,*
> As techeth art of speche hem that it leere. (V (F), 100–4)

The feelings aroused in us by the general comic duality in Book II of *The House of Fame* are varied and subtle, only fully explored and described by the poem itself. The clash of feeling which is amusement is caused by the difference between our response to the *persona* and our response to the real Chaucer. It will be more satisfactory and more accurate, however, since we have never had the pleasure of fully knowing the real Chaucer, to say that our response to the real Chaucer is our response to the whole art of the poem, to the speeches of all the characters, the description, the arrangement of events, the ironies of expression, to all the voices of the poetry. We must not identify this response with our response to the Eagle alone, for the Eagle is himself a comic character, with his own duality. We read the words attributed to the Eagle, as to the *persona*, with the special comic dual consciousness.

It is most difficult, and I attempt it with the greatest hesitancy, to attach a label to the feelings aroused in us. We err if we think that there are a number of fairly clearly defined human feelings, love, hate, friendship, and so on. These are only the most general categories of feeling. There are an infinite number of feelings, and no feeling is unmixed. Every time we love we love in a different way. In literature, every successful love-poem even within the same convention describes a slightly different kind of love; every successful comic poem within the same convention a slightly different kind of comic complex. Every work of literature may be regarded as an attempt at definition of feeling through creation, which is one of the many reasons why criticism can never usurp on poetry, and one of the many temptations which beset a critic to throw up his pen and say ' Oh, read the poem yourself! ' And yet, having learnt so much from hearing other people's responses, even when disagreeing with them, it may still be worth while to go on to attempt to explain and justify one's own, however inadequately.

Most briefly and generally, then, it seems to me, we feel in Book II of *The House of Fame* sympathetic inferiority associated with the *persona*, and sympathetic superiority, associated with the poem as a whole. The very first humorous passage illustrates the inferiority-superiority complex, and is also a good example of the need we have to be careful in detailed explanations. The Eagle has just swept up the Chaucer-*persona* (a clumsy expression, but necessary to remind us of the ever present duality in Chaucer's presentation of himself), and the poem goes on,

> Thus I longe in hys clawes lay,
> Til at the laste he to me spak
> In mannes vois, and seyde, "Awak!
> And be not agast so, for shame!"
> And called me tho by my name,
> And, for I shulde the bet abreyde,
> Me mette, "Awak," to me he seyde,
> Ryght in the same vois and stevene
> That useth oon I koude nevene;
> And with that vois, soth for to seyn,
> My mynde cam to me ageyn,
> For hyt was goodly seyd to me,
> So nas hyt never wont to be.   (ll. 554–66)

Here, where the general build-up of the whole complex begins, we have a clear superiority-inferiority
situation. The incongruity lies in the superiority attributed to a lower order of being, a bird, and the
inferiority attributed to the naturally superior being,
the man. So that the general duality is built upon
two specific dualities. There is another duality. The
Awak! is kindly, and contrasts with an unkindly one
more familiar to the poet. There is another : for the
Eagle is compared with the usual speaker of the *Awak!*,
who must be human, and again the natural order is
reversed, for the bird is shown as superior to the human
being. Now, it is also clear that Chaucer's audience
must clearly have known who the human being was ;
it is a private joke, and better for the original audience
than for us, since they knew the personality concerned,
as we never can. It is often assumed that the person
referred to was Chaucer's wife. This is perfectly
possible, and would refer to a naturally comic duality
—the naturally superior husband (according to medieval
English and modern Japanese thought), forced into a
position of inferiority by his wife. Chaucer refers to
such a situation with the Host in *The Canterbury Tales.*
But is it so likely in the courtly situation of this poem
that Chaucer's reference is to his wife ? Such a reference is probable enough in lower-middle class do-
mesticity, but much less likely in Chaucer's own circumstances. Would not such a joke about his wife
have seemed in rather poor taste ? Once this doubt is
sown, we may note that the Eagle speaks ' in mannes
vois '. This might mean no more than ' human voice ',

but the natural meaning would be ' the voice of a man ' ; in which case the reference could easily be to the marshal, who was responsible for the discipline of the Squires of the Royal Household, of whom Chaucer was one for many years.   The marshal would have been known to all the audience, and what we may well have here is not a sort of nineteenth-century music hall joke about ' the missus ', but the kind of joke that might be made about a little loved serjeant-major.

Whatever the truth of it may be, the Eagle goes on to say that the Chaucer-*persona* is difficult to carry— presumably because he is wriggling with fear—and comforts him.   Therewith,

> " O God ! " thoughte I, " that madest kynde,
> Shal I noon other weyes dye ?
> Wher Joves wol me stellyfye . . .?
> I neyther am Ennok, ne Elye, *etc.*   (ll. 584–8)

This is a variant on the superiority-inferiority clash, in which Chaucer compares himself with those in Biblical and classical antiquity who were swept up into the heavens.   The *persona* is represented as being extremely conceited (comparing himself to stellified heroes and others singularly favoured by God) and at the same time, because he is so silly and so frightened, as singularly lacking in grounds for conceit.   Here is one humorous clash.   But the *persona* is not the real Chaucer, as is suggested in the line closely following,

> Loo, this was thoo my fantasye !   (l. 593)

Such a line invites us apparently to laugh at the poet himself, but there is a difference.   When a man says,

'How absurd I was!', by the very words he is separating himself from his own absurdity, and inviting us to laugh not only at the absurdity itself, but also at the contrast between his detached, sensible, 'real' self, which notices the absurdity, and his former self, which did not notice the absurdity. That is what Chaucer is doing with his comment here. A comment like this is more open than is usual with Chaucer. As his art matures he leaves us to appreciate the difference between his *persona* and his real self without being prodded or nudged. He can the more easily afford to do this because of his own immediate and intimate relation with his primary audience. But some later readers have taken the *persona*, especially in his naivety, for the real Chaucer, while others have fallen into the opposite trap of taking everything that Chaucer says as possessing a double meaning.

The interest now begins to shift to the Eagle, or rather, to what the Eagle says. First, the Eagle comments on Chaucer's way of life. For a full appreciation of the humour we lack the essential knowledge of the real Chaucer's life. It must have been fairly like the Eagle's description, or there would be no point in the description—complete discrepancy would have been merely silly. Yet there must have been some discrepancy if there was any humour. In fact, the note of slight exaggeration in the text, the mild contempt (e.g. 1. 621) with which the Eagle treats the Chaucer-*persona*, the general drift of meaning, all suggest that the real Chaucer's life was different from the description. Although the accurate dating of the poem is difficult, it must have

been written in a period when, although principally
occupied at the Customs House, Chaucer had, or had
recently had, journeys abroad on important diplomatic
matters. No doubt there were other activities in court
and City. The full humour of the passage must have
consisted in the way the *persona* agrees with and yet
contrasts with, the real Chaucer. We can only guess
at this through the tone of the passage.

The Eagle then moves on to his lecture, of which the
humour is only partly concerned with my present subject, on Chaucer himself as a subject of humour. In
brief the humour of the lecture is based on an incongruity between means and end. The means are well-
known, up-to-date scientific concepts, all perfectly good
for the times; the end is pure fantasy. The whole is
an intellectual joke, solemn-faced; the enjoyment of
pseudo-science. It is the first treatment of learning as
a subject of humour, which I shall comment on later.
The modern English equivalents are Pope's and Swift's
Scriblerus Papers, or the pseudo-scientific footnotes of
the *Dunciad*, or, to come to the present day, the various
delightfully pseudo-learned ingenuities of Mr. Stephen
Potter. The relationship of the Eagle to the Chaucer-
persona is however maintained, and its essentially
dramatic quality enhances the humour of the lecture.
The bird and the poet become lecturer and pupil at the
same time; as the bird soars in body, so he drags the
mind of the pupil after him. Contrast after contrast
opens out, within unity. A bird is a lecturer. A
lecture is given at a vast height above the earth. A
victim is lectured at : a lecturee (if I may use the word)

is a victim. The victim's fear contrasts with the
Eagle's self-confidence and self-delight. The victim's
brief, tense replies contrast with the lengthy exposition
of the Eagle. The Eagle's own self-complacency is
mildly amusing in the light of all these contrasts, and
because of the implicit contrast between any talking
animal or bird, and a human being.

One might go further in detailed exposition, but enough
has been said. To sum up: the general bases of the
comic duality here are the clash between the Chaucer-
persona and the real Chaucer: within this we may
detect a complex inferiority-superiority conflict, centr-
ing partly on the contrast between the real Chaucer and
the *persona*, and partly on the contrast between the
Eagle and the Chaucer-*persona*. The general flow of
feeling is more sympathetic than antipathetic. No
doubt we feel some limitation of sympathy towards the
persona : we look down on him, and that implies contempt; we look down on the *persona* and look up to the
poet who is pretending to be the *persona*. The faults
of the *persona* are not serious: they are indeed comfortable faults, and allow us to feel superior, to feel ourselves on the side of the Eagle in fact, and, in a curious
way, on the side of the real Chaucer. Yet we are not
entirely on the side of the real Chaucer, because he is
pretending to be the *persona*. The reader is caught
up in this complicated relationship between real Chaucer
and *persona*, as if he were between two mirrors set up
opposite each other, which reflect each other infinitely.
He sympathises, so to say, on both sides. One can
sympathetically share the *persona's* nervousness at his

aerial journey, and also, with relief, feel superior to the *persona* for feeling nervous. That is the pleasure of humour; you can have your cake and eat it too.

The comic conflict is fairly well balanced in the poem, and consequently so are the conflicting responses. One feeling does not predominate. There is instead a pleasurable gentle flux of mild, mostly sympathetic feelings, which leaves us with the agreeable sensations of not too violent exercise in a beautiful and friendly green countryside, on a sunny afternoon. This is not to be despised. The sea is no less the sea when the breeze is no hurricane, and when the waves flash no more than serves to break the calm, and the air sparkles. On the other hand, the poem is not relaxed. You need your wits about you, and there is a pleasurable employment of the mind.

In *The Book of the Duchess* Chaucer found it a convenient device for furthering the action to make his *persona* ignorant. The ignorance in that poem was essentially accidental, though the *persona* is also represented as slow to understand—more, one feels, as a narrative device than as a conscious representation of character. In *The House of Fame* the *persona* is for the first time represented as positively dull-witted. The *persona* in *The House of Fame* is also for the first time represented, not merely as unsuccessful in love (as in *The Book of the Duchess* and a thousand other medieval poems) but also as ignorant of love. This is highly unusual. I cannot remember any other medieval poet who thus represents himself. The ignorance is amusing, for it contrasts with the whole art and nature of the poem, as we see again in *The Parliament of Fowls*, which follows next. Before coming to that great poem, however, we may notice that Book III of *The House of Fame* makes no use of the comic possibilities of the *persona*. Chaucer reverts to a more conventional usage.

IV

The Parliament of Fowls

The Parliament of Fowls presents a *persona* of the poet who is ignorant and fearful about love, but much interested in it. The poem presents several aspects of love, developing out of and contrasting with each other. The various aspects of love are not in themselves humorous because they are not sufficiently closely united. The principal aim of the poem is not a humorous treatment of its principal subject, which is love. But the poem is remarkable for its lightness of touch and there is specific humour in Chaucer's presentation of himself, and in parts of the birds' debate, when for the first time humour is connected with class-distinction.

After so lengthy an analysis of the humorous treatment of himself in *The House of Fame*, little need be said of the same subject in *The Parliament*, where it is much less important. The relationship between the Eagle and the *persona* is paralleled by that between Scipio Africanus and the *persona*. Scipio adopts much the same sharpness of manner as the Eagle did to his charge. The comic situation does not depend so much here on the reversals of related superiority-inferiority. The humour rests rather on the *persona's* conflicting

attitudes towards love; ignorance and fear are balanced
against great interest in the first two stanzas, and again,
fear beats against eagerness when he is confronted by
the two messages on the gate to the park:

These vers of gold and blak iwriten were,
Of whiche I gan astoned to beholde,
For with that oon encresede ay my fere,
And with that other gan myn herte bolde;
That oon me hette, that other dide me colde:
No wit hadde I, for errour, for to chese,
To entre or flen, or me to save or lese.

Right as, betwixen adamauntes two
Of evene myght, a pece of yren set
Ne hath no myght to meve to ne fro—
For what that oon may hale, that other let—
Ferde I, that nyste whether me was bet
To entre or leve, til Affrycan, my gide,
Me hente, and shof in at the gates wide.   (ll. 141–54)

This is no bad illustration of the very nature of humour:
a tension between opposing forces, with a final movement
in one direction or another. It may also be added
that while the humour of the *persona*'s predicament
when he is pushed into the park is based on a dignity-
indignity duality, the word *shof* did not have its modern,
colloquial, undignified, associations.

The function of the slight figure of the *persona* in
the poem as a whole is to link together the various
aspects of love. The mild humour with which he is
treated is sufficient to lighten the tone of the poem, to
keep balance, to preserve a judicial sense of *pro* and *con*,
so that he can dip on the one side into elements of

philosophy and on the other into luxury, or satire. As
so often with Chaucer, by sacrificing the extremes he
can include an immensely varied range of more middling
matters—in social class, in feeling, in thought.

The birds' debate is a good example of this balanced
mixture of the poem. It is also a case for the exercise
of tact. Some critics, knowing Chaucer is a humorist,
and seeing that there is some humour in some parts of
the debate, assume that everything is meant to be
funny or at least ironical. It is essential to realise in
humour as in every other complicated emotional state,
that the tension must not, indeed cannot, be kept up
equally all the way through. There must be variety of
pace, of material. We cannot be at a stretch for long
periods of time. The nineteenth- and twentieth-century
exaggeration of the importance of the short poem has
distorted our views, assumptions and expectations of
literature in many ways, and in none more than its assumption that poetry must be at a high pitch of feeling
and meaning in every line and word to be successful.
On the contrary we need bread as much as cake. In
a humorous poem we need not expect to find humour
in every line. Especially in *The Parliament* we must
remember that the poem is not primarily humorous.

The debate begins with Nature making an opening
speech. Then three hawks each state their love for,
and claim as a reward, the same formel. This provokes
a long argument between them (not recorded) and
finally, the lower birds impatiently break in. It is
arranged that the terslet will give the opinion of the
birds of prey on the subject, the goose will speak for

waterfowl, the cuckoo for worm-eating fowl, the turtle-dove for seed-eating fowl.

We must now make ourselves clear on some matters that have become confused. First, class-distinctions in love had been early recognised in the French thir-teenth-century love-visions whose tradition the *Parlia-ment* follows.* Birds would debate questions of love, and the birds to a limited extent represented social classes. That is, hawks always represent the knightly class. I know of no case where lower birds represent other *specific* classes, but they vaguely represent differ-ent levels of society. The reason for this vagueness is that there was no medieval theory distinguishing people into purely social classes. The only theory of class distinction was that which divided men into knights (i.e. the class responsible for defence of all and the maintenance of justice); clergy (responsible for the spiritual well-being of all); ploughmen (responsible for food-production and general labour for all). It is clear that the knights of medieval theory coincided with the higher levels of society, but the division into clergy and ploughmen corresponded only very approximately to the many different levels and social groups found especially in the medieval town. There was no room for townsfolk in this medieval class-theory, which was indeed more of an ideal for society than any expression of what men actually saw in society. Unless birds had represented clergy and ploughmen (neither especially relevant in this poem) there were no specific categories

* See my article in *Eigo-Seinen*, May and June 1957.

birds could represent. So, in the French love-visions, the vague sense of the classification of society finds an equally vague counterpart in the division of birds into representatives of the knightly class and a flock of other birds, some of whom speak on behalf of the *vilains*, or common man. In some French poems the birds divide otherwise, some favouring knights and others favouring the clergy. But in Chaucer the matter is not so simple. He, like other poets, had no categories of thought into which he could fit the variety of classes which he was conscious of in London especially, with Westminster and the Court near, and all the variety of great and small produced by a complex commercial system. But he was obviously very much aware of these different classes or groups as above all else *The General Prologue to the Canterbury Tales* shows us. One may guess that Chaucer's special sensitivity to difference of class springs from the process of his own family's rise (in which he was not the latest nor the highest), from very middle middleclass origins, as we now see them, to positions of wealth and national responsibility and finally, in his grand-daughter, to the rank of an earldom. Chaucer must have been conscious of the difference between his own position in the court of Richard II, and that of his grandfather's status in life.

In the *Parliament* he clearly divides the birds into groups. And we feel (though of course our class-feeling is sharper than Chaucer's in some ways) that these groups correspond to the classes of men. I am sure we are right—so long as we do not try to work out a table of exact correspondences for which there is not

a shred of clear historical evidence; we must not, for
example, from some fancied resemblance make the seed-
fowl represent 'the merchant class'. This is to consider too curiously. The classification of the birds
unquestionably rests in detail on the entirely natural
and scientific (if erroneous) classification which Chaucer
found in the encyclopaedia of Vincent of Beauvais.
The natural classification *only symbolises* the classes of
men : the hawks as always represent the knightly class, but
the water-, worm- and seed-fowl do not represent other
specific classes. There were none in Chaucer's conscious mind for them to represent.

The next question is Chaucer's attitude to the various
groups. This is better tackled by taking very briefly
his attitude to the various individuals. There need
be no confusion here between Chaucer's *persona* and
his real opinion. The *persona* is not writing the poem,
and impersonal comments need not be attributed to the
persona and then discounted. Thus, when the poem
refers to 'the fol kokkow', we can take it for granted that
the cuckoo is meant to be thought of as a fool, with no
irony intended. (This seems obvious enough, but
there are interpreters who appear to assume that Chaucer
thinks the cuckoo speaks good sense.) Again, when
the poem refers to the noise goose and cuckoo and others
make, the noise is called 'lewednesse' (l. 520), i.e.
ignorance (and here *is* clearly implied ignorance of
good behaviour, of what is proper). The most contemptuous phrasing is reserved for the water-fowl and
the goose (ll. 554–60). On the other hand the hawks
are treated everywhere with respect. Compare the

dignity of the diction in which the election of the tersel
as spokesman is described (ll. 526–32) with the stanza
already referred to describing the election of the goose
by the water-fowl. Nature herself describes the first
tersel as the most worthy that is there, and the others
are to choose in order of rank (ll. 393–401). There can
be no doubt that Nature, the deputy of God, represents
all that is good, and her approval of the order of the
birds, and implicitly therefore of the order of society,
is significant. Chaucer was orthodox. Not for him
the rhyme, sung by the suffering and discontented
peasants of his time

> When Adam delved and Eve span
> Who was then the gentleman?

Chaucer fully approved, at least in theory, of the
class-structure of the society of his day, as indeed one
would have expected. And he was also, we may say,
in view of the way he distinguishes the groups of birds
more clearly than any other poet, unusually sensitive
to the real, though intellectually unrecognised, class-
distinctions of his day.

We are now to examine the speeches and the quality
of humour of the debate. There is no humour in the
presentation of the speech by the first suitor. It is comparatively long, and elaborate, and quite orthodox in
its expression of love. Its content and occasionally
its very phrasing can be matched in several short poems
written by Chaucer, and the content in general is just
what we should expect from the development of *fine
amour* in England at this time. It is clear also that

as always in England, if we could transpose bird into
man, his aim would be marriage. The medieval Nature
does not encourage adulterous unions, and Chaucer's
source for Nature, the *De Planctu Naturae* written by
Alanus de Insulis, makes this perfectly explicit, if we
want more proof than that she is the deputy of the
medieval Christian God. In the following speeches by
the second and third suitors, it is again almost impossible to find, as some critics claim to do, anything
comic. Where is the basis of incongruity? It is not
true, as any wide reading of courtly French medieval
love-poetry will show, (and as I shall point out in a
forthcoming edition of the *Parliament*) that they express
unusual, and therefore incongruous sentiments.

It is of course quite possible for a modern reader,
Western or Japanese, to find the suitors' speeches comic.
The basis of his amusement will be the incongruity
between the love-sentiments which the eagles express,
and those we ourselves feel to be appropriate in such
a situation. Such humour is clearly not Chaucer's,
but the result of time and change.

There is equally no humour in the opinion expressed
by the tersel eagle on behalf of birds of prey. Humour
begins when the goose is elected to speak. Here the
comic incongruity arises in the hasty and undignified,
talkative way (*golee*, l. 556, a ' throat-ful ', is a contemptuous word) in which the election is made, contrasted with the decency with which elections ought to
be conducted, and with the way the birds of prey conducted theirs a few lines before. The essence of the
goose's solution is

But she wol love hym, lat hym love another! (l. 567)

which provokes a contemptuous comment from the sparrowhawk, and

The laughter aros of gentil foules alle. (l. 575)

From what I have said of Nature's approval of the structure of society, which of course implies Chaucer's own approval, and his identification of himself with the point of view of the ' gentles ', it is obvious that the real Chaucer also thinks the goose's solution is so wrong as to be funny. This impression is heightened by the speech of the turtle-dove immediately following, who says

Nay, God forbede a lovere shulde chaunge! (l. 582)

And it should be noted that the turtle is also one of the lower classes. The duck and the cuckoo, both contemptuously treated, add solutions equally wrong and foolish, but ' the perfect reason of the goose ' will serve as example of the humour involved.

The goose's opinion is worth dwelling on, because the convention of love has so changed. The goose in saying ' if the formel won't love him, let him love some-one who will ', appears to many modern men to be expressing the merest common-sense. The convention changed long before our day. In *Twelfth Night* when the Duke finds Olivia really out of his grasp, because she has married Sebastian, he turns with ease to Viola. But Shakespeare has prepared us for this a long way back in the play in all sorts of ways, and manages the change with great tact. Now, we may say that the Duke's way is the most sensible. But if we take the

situation in the *Parliament* it surely argues great ignorance of human nature to suppose that a man can easily
turn from love and reverence of one woman to that of
another.   Experience aside, literature is full of stories
of people who just could not do that, however sensible
they might agree it was.   Nor is this a question of *fine
amour* and the European tradition.   *The Great Gatsby*
is, among other things, such a story of compulsive love.
The goose is guilty of an absurdity.   The image of
love she presents is absurdly incongruous with love as
we know it in life and books.

There is also the more detailed point of *fine amour*.
Each of the suitors has sworn on his honour that his
love is everlasting.   The goose is recommending a
course not only unnatural but dishonourable.

The comic incongruity of the goose lies partly in the
incongruity of her idea of love with the true one.   The
incongruity evokes feelings of warm sympathy for true
love in conflict with sharp antipathy for the goose's
idea.   But though there is some basis for humour here,
the two responses are not sufficiently closely united for
the humour to be very intense.   The goose is also comic
because of the way she is presented.   She has ' facounde
gent ', ' nice ' eloquence.   *Gent* is a word always used
mockingly by Chaucer after the very early *Romaunt*.
And when the goose begins to speak there is an element
of mimicry in Chaucer's representation of her speech.
Mimicry is a good example of the essentially dual nature
of humour : when a man is mimicked by someone else,
the result is sure to be humorous in itself, even if the
man is not absurd, because of the clash between the

two images of him that are presented, his true self and the mimicry. If the mimicry is an exaggerated copy, while still bearing a close resemblance to the original, the humour is greater because the incongruity is greater, though still firmly based on unity.

The goose is also amusing because of her bustling self-importance. The comic incongruity here is between her own estimate of herself and ours.

The result is that our response to the goose is a mixture of sensations: she is contemptible, but not dangerous; we respond to the mimicry of a goose's ' speech ' in human language; and we always have a fellow-feeling, as well as hostility, for self-importance. One element more: I have maintained that Chaucer thought the goose's opinion unnatural and dishonourable, and that so should we. That does not mean that Chaucer was incapable of sympathising with the goose's opinion to some extent. The fact that the goose's solution seems sensible at first sight to us does not mean that it necessarily seemed so to Chaucer, but having regard to the common chances and necessities of life it is unlikely that Chaucer, consciously or unconsciously, completely condemned the goose's opinion. It is a natural error. There is therefore a conflict in our attitude to the goose between sympathy and antipathy. There is in this case more antipathy than sympathy, and Chaucer's humour is hostile. I repeat that it is not *essential* for humour to be kindly. Chaucer is kindly in his mockery of himself, but not of the goose. And his attitude to duck and cuckoo is much the same as to the goose.

The relation of the humour of goose, duck and cuckoo to the class situation is indirect. First, we may note that it is only the representatives of the lower-classes who are ignorant and wrong about the nature of love. The knightly class has only right feeling. Secondly, however, not *all* the representatives of the lower classes are ignorant and wrong about the nature of love : the turtle-dove is at one with the eagles. Chaucer therefore does not regard the lower-classes as necessarily wrong, or contemptible, or ridiculous, in themselves. But he regards them as peculiarly liable to go astray. Three out of their four representatives are ignorant, coarse, and selfish in their attitudes to the finer feelings. The greatness of Chaucer, and partly the source of his humour here, is that for all his general hostility to their ideas and attitudes, he presents them in such a way that we cannot but, to an admittedly limited extent, sympathise with them, even while disapproving. Nevertheless, we do disapprove, and we disapprove because the lower-classes seem peculiarly liable to go against God's law of Nature, to be hostile to order, and thus by implication, to the upper classes ; in other words, because they are liable to be subversive. It is interesting to compare here a penetrating remark made by George Orwell about the humour of Dickens :

> A joke worth laughing at always has an idea behind it, and usually a subversive idea. Dickens is able to go on being funny because he is in revolt against authority, and authority is always there to be laughed at.
>
> (*Critical Essays*, 2nd edition, 1951, p. 56)

This is true of Dickens. But with Chaucer it is the opposite of the truth. Chaucer is able to go on being funny because he is always on the side of authority, and subversion is always there to be laughed at. The ideas behind Chaucer's jokes are usually authoritative ideas.

We are if anything too well accustomed these days to the idea (more or less true since the end of the eighteenth century) that the great artist is ' naturally ' in rebellion against society ; the artist as Outsider. The reverse is true of Chaucer (and, we might add, of Shakespeare and Samuel Johnson as well, to go no further). Chaucer is very eminently an example of the great artist as the Insider. This does not mean, of course, that he was uncritical of his own society— what sensible man is ? But conscious as he was of abuses and miseries and misfortunes, he still approved of the established order as it could and should be. He was no rebel. He was for law and order, with their divine sanctions. And yet he sees no need for authority always to be solemn, any more than Dickens saw any need for subversion to be.

The humour in *The House of Fame* and *The Parliament of Fowls* need not be over-emphasised. It is valuable however to study it in some detail because it is comparatively simple, and because it will give a groundwork for understanding the later, riper humour, which is more complex. It also affords us the beginning of a view of the development of Chaucer's humour, and thus of his whole literary imagination.

V

The Canterbury Tales

The works which immediately follow *The House of Fame* and *The Parliament* are not remarkable for their humour. In *Boece, Troilus and Criseyde, The Legend of Good Women, The Knight's Tale*, there is indeed (apart from *Boece*) a sense of humour occasionally to be traced; but of the subjects of comedy there is little. We then come to the full flowering of *The Canterbury Tales*, where detailed chronology is almost impossible, and where the humour is extremely rich, subtle, and complex.

The subjects of Chaucer's humour dealt with up to now have been himself, a little of the humour of learning (in the Eagle's lecture) and, in a special sense, humour arising out of class-distinction. *The Canterbury Tales* reveal these subjects much developed, and add to them the subjects of women and ' hypocrisy ', besides some minor subjects, many of which may be summed up under the heading of ' physical rough-and-tumble '. The physical rough-and-tumble is the simplest sort of humour, when a drunken man falls off his horse, or a wife trying to help her husband in a fight gives him a stunning crack on the head, or a lover gets into the wrong bed, or a man expecting to kiss a girl's face finds the reverse, or another man trying to make him repeat this trick gets badly burnt, and so on. Most of these incidents and others like them Chaucer found in his sources; he did not usually invent them. They can be summed up in such terms as ' the biter bit ', ' the tables turned '; they represent the incongruities arising out of reversal which are beloved in folk literature, where Chaucer usually found them. They are in essence simple, and their appeal is universal. By combining them with subtler kinds of humour Chaucer achieves a mastery of humour perhaps unequalled. At their best the humour of the tales ranges from broadest farce to subtlest comedy, from powerful satire to gentlest and kindliest mockery. The broad farce at the end of *The Miller's Tale* and *The Reeve's Tale* comes as a glorious climax to a long build-up of the complex patterns of feelings.

Before touching the new subjects of humour it will be best to discuss more briefly those we have already met. The earliest subject of Chaucer's humour was himself, as seen through the distorting *persona* of an overworked, dull-witted man, unlucky in love. Something recognisably similar appears in *The Canterbury Tales* when the Host calls on Chaucer himself for a tale (VII, 691 ff.) The Host describes Chaucer as downward looking, rather serious (since he tells him to look up pleasantly); fat; ' elvyssh ' (i.e. mysterious, ' different '), in face; and having to do with no-one. Chaucer represents himself as saying that he knows only one tale in rhyme, and then proceeds to tell *Sir Thopas*. Since this is the one tale in the whole collection which is thought by the Host to be downright bad, there is obvious comedy in this, depending as usual on the incongruity between the *persona* and the real Chaucer. The real Chaucer is telling all the tales, and is speaking even through the Host, whereas the *persona*, whom the real Chaucer pretends to be, is hopelessly old-fashioned and incompetent at telling a tale. But the tale itself is an extremely clever parody, both social and literary, and the *persona* described by the Host is a good deal more dignified than he who was swept up by the Eagle. One might say that Chaucer has by now, as we might expect, a great deal more self-confidence, less need to be, so to speak, self-depreciating. This impression is confirmed when after the brilliantly absurd *Sir Thopas* the Chaucer-*persona* goes on to tell *The Tale of Melibeus*, a long, long tract on various moral problems. Some critics have maintained that just as there are some sorrows too deep for tears, so there are some jokes too deep for laughter. We will not quibble about the laughter; there may be some jokes too deep to be funny, but the human mind is not so constituted as to recognise them. The *Melibeus* is not funny. Can we *possibly* imagine that Chaucer was so far from his usual self when he wrote it (which must have taken weeks or months) that he *thought* it was funny? To think so is to deny any possibility of sensible criticism. The *Melibeus* is not funny and was not meant to be. It is a perfectly serious contribution to problems which may even interest us now, such as the justification and abolition of war. That the Chaucer-*persona* tells it is certainly an inconsistency in character, just as the *Melibeus* itself, with its immense length and the nature of its subject-matter, is a major inconsistency within what is never more than the superficial realism of the whole *Canterbury Tales*. But that also clearly shows Chaucer less divided within himself. Humour about himself fades as Chaucer gets older.

The humour of literature and learning was in *The*

House of Fame closely associated with humour about himself, and the association is maintained, as already suggested, in *The Canterbury Tales* with the story of *Sir Thopas*. But with *Sir Thopas* only a small part of the humour is concerned with the relation of the *persona* to the tale. The other sources of the comic in *Sir Thopas* are more important: the literary parody and hence satire of the old-fashioned English tail-rhyme romance; and the social satire of the Flemish knights. *Sir Thopas* therefore is an example of humour of class-distinction, as of literature; but the two run together, for it is clear from other evidence that the old tail-rhyme romances had long ceased to be thought well of by the sophisticated modern taste of Chaucer's circle, and had almost certainly come to be associated with the less sophisticated taste of what we might now call the lower middle-classes.

A similar example of the humour of literature going along with the humour of class-distinction comes in a much more elaborate and complex poem: *The Miller's Tale*, one of the greatest poems Chaucer wrote, perpetually amusing, perpetually enriching to read. The complexities start from the dramatic situation, in which the tale is supposed to be spoken by the Miller, and in the way it annoys the Reeve. But while noting this, which helps to build up the complex of feeling, we must concentrate on the poem itself, which is in no way stylistically or psychologically suited to the speaker.

The literary humour of the poem lies in its use of outworn clichés of popular poetry (as was pointed out some years ago in a little-known essay by Mr. E. T.

Donaldson), and in the way in which Alison and to some extent Absolon are portrayed in relation to the standard literary tradition of portraiture. Words like *hende* (l. 3199), *gent* (l. 3234), *lemman* (l. 3278) and a few others were those of the old rather provincial English poetry of the early fourteenth-century, like The Harley Lyrics, and the tail-rhyme romances. The love-declaration of ' hende Nicholas ' is full of them, and his very love-making is a coarse cheerful lustful debased copy of the words and desires of a knight professing *fine amour*. It might be called a parody of *fine amour* but that a parody is usually understood to mock the genuine thing it copies, whereas here, it is the copy which is mocked. We are well used to the mocking copy : it is less frequent to find in English the mocked copy. The difference is similar to the difference between Dickens and Chaucer in their attitude to authority. Chaucer again shows us the artist as Insider. In real life, certainly in English social life, it is very common for the upper classes to mock at the lower classes, but since the upper classes rarely produce literature, we have very few examples of such mockery. One of the rare modern cases is that of Sir Max Beerbohm, particularly in the parody *Scruts* in *A Christmas Garland*, where for example he is much amused that a poor man should use a raincoat for an overcoat. Chaucer is funnier, and did not, incidentally, find poverty or the shifts of poverty, amusing at all.

The relation of the portrayals of Alison and Absolon to the literary tradition is similar to the relationship of the love sentiments in *The Miller's Tale* to *fine amour*.

The custom of formal portraiture of hero and heroine, and their type of beauty, derive ultimately from classical antiquity but became elaborated in special medieval form in the Latin and French poetry of the twelfth century.* To take the heroine as an example ; she is usually tall, her hair is golden, forehead white, eyebrows black, thin and curved ; her eyes are usually said to be like stars, her nose is well-proportioned, her teeth white, lips red, her complexion red and white. Her breath smells sweetly. This is the type of the beauty of the heroine of poetry all over Europe from the twelfth to the six-teenth or seventeenth centuries. Her most radiant appearance in art (where her figure, with slender shoulders and small waist but rather swelling belly, is exactly according to the favoured ' vital statistics ') is the Venus of Botticelli.

This ideal of feminine beauty so constant and wide-spread in time and place provides a very good example of a convention. It was so powerful that even in a country where most women are very dark, like Italy, its golden-haired ideal held unquestioned sway. It was the only way in which a heroine could be imagined. The use made of this conventional ideal by various writers is therefore a matter of much interest. In England, Shakespeare and Donne are the earliest I have noted reacting against the convention. Chaucer ac-cepts it fully.

Chaucer's description of Alison, however, shows an

* Detailed evidence will be found in my article on ' The Idea of Feminine Beauty,' *Modern Language Review* (1955), pp. 257 ff., and C. Schaar, *The Golden Mirror*, Lund, 1956.

interesting characteristic use of the convention. She
is a caricature, but the joke is on her, not on the convention. Here is a carpenter's wife, a luscious but also
loose, tartish creature, described as if she were a heroine.
Thus her forehead is white—when she has washed it
after her work (l. 3310); heroines did not do housework, and could hardly be thought of as getting dirty.
Alison's eyebrows are curved, black and thin, like a
true beauty's, but they were thin because they were
plucked ('ypulled', l. 3245), and Chaucer's own ad-
dition of praise to Beute in the part of *Le Roman de la
Rose* which he translated was that she did not pluck her
eyebrows (*Romaunt*, l. 1018). I have noted these details
and others elsewhere; there is no need to repeat more.
A modern reader need not be well-read in courtly Latin
and French poetry to understand Chaucer's attitude
to Alison, for no one could think the comparisons with
which her beauty is described are entirely serious—
weasel, swallow, calf or kid. She is called by the
contemptuous names ' popelote ' and ' wench '. But
to appreciate the richness of the portrait, and its cleverness, it is certainly desirable to have some knowledge
of the literary tradition, though one need go no further
for it than the portrait of Blanche in Chaucer's own
Book of the Duchess.

The literary humour of *The Miller's Tale* is only part
of the full humour of the poem, yet it is in itself very
complex. The comic duality lies in implicitly remind-
ing us of the true, respected, rhetorical, literary tradition, and giving an adept distortion of it. Our feelings
are divided between respect and contempt; and also

in this case yet again, between superiority and inferiority in literary taste. The quality of feeling is mildly patronising and contemptuous. The comic duality is also poetically rich. The bright image of the heroine is raised in our minds, and though Alison is vulgar in comparison, she borrows brightness from the comparison. The natural feeling for a heroine is an idealising reverence. We feel no more reverence for Alison than Nicholas does (cf. l. 3275), but there is release of the tension of ideality in the very sexiness of Alison. And her sexiness is attractive, too. Here the approach to *The Miller's Tale* through the literary humour begins to broaden out, as is right and inevitable, into more general considerations, which, however, are better discussed later under other subjects.

The most strikingly comic use of literature and learning occurs in *The Nun's Priest's Tale*. The incongruity is inherent in a tale of talking animals or birds, but not all such tales are funny. Chaucer's is funny because the bird-like character of the bird and the incongruously learned nature of his talk are both emphasised. At the same time the talk is closely related to the bird's own situation; the discussion of dreams, love, and predestination arise out of the definite and so to say reasonable anxieties of a cock who has dreamt of a threatening fox. This is the same kind of intellectual humour as is found in Book II of *The House of Fame*, a sport of the mind. That exercise that we are accustomed to take in deep seriousness we now take knowing that there is no important end—and we feel satisfaction and a release of tension from that knowledge.

Just as when playing cards for trivial stakes, or playing or watching a game of football, our feelings operate as if the stakes, or as if winning, were important; so in Chaucer's poem, we follow with interest the line of the argument as if the conclusion were important, knowing the end to be trivial. In this kind of humour there is a good deal of straightforward intellectual interest—and intellectual interest is quite as much an emotion as any of the varieties of love, though we lack names for it.

The most famous piece of humour in *The Nun's Priest's Tale* is the rhetorical exclamation with which Chaucer bursts out when the fox has seized Chauntecleer:

> O Gaufred, deere maister soverayn,
> That whan thy worthy kyng Richard was slayn
> With shot, compleynedest his deeth so soore,
> Why ne hadde I now thy sentence and thy loore,
> The Friday for to chide, as diden ye?
> For on a Friday, soothly, slayn was he.
> Thanne wolde I shewe yow how that I koude pleyne
> For Chauntecleres drede and for his peyne.
>
> (VII, 3347–54)

The reference is to the famous master of rhetoric, Geoffrey of Vinsauf, who in his *Nova Poetria* gave instructions how to write poetry, and included by way of example his own lament for the death of his lord, King Richard I, the Lionheart. Geoffrey's lament is frigid and artificial to a degree. The comic contrasts in Chaucer's outburst are rich. First his praise of Geoffrey is ironical. The exaggerated praise contrasts with the adverse criticism that is implied, and points to a further comic contrast in Geoffrey himself—the man who tells others how to perform what he signally fails to do himself; the man who is absurdly conceited about his own failure, which he regards as success. Chaucer also points more specifically to Geoffrey's absurdity in ' chiding the Friday ', in treating a day of the week, that is, as a person, and again he heightens our sense of the absurdity by saying he wishes he could do it himself. Chaucer's own lament is also absurd in a way that Geoffrey's is not, for all this extravagant high style is devoted to a low and trivial subject; and the farmyard cock, already a subject of complicated and sophisticated humour is absurdly compared with the ' worthy king Richard '. Our feelings are complicated in response to these complex contrasts: genuine respect for the ' dear master sovereign ' is checked by contempt, solemnity by frivolity, sadness by carefree interest. The lighter feelings obviously prevail. If we felt no sadness at all for King Richard (and the original audience would presumably, being so much nearer him, have felt more spontaneously for him than we do) there would be no humour, because no clash of feeling. But of sadness there is no more than a trace left by the mention of death; we are only really conscious of Chauntecleer, already a comic figure, and the flow of cheerful feeling is far greater than the very small touch of sadness. There seems to be little question of kindness or unkindness towards Chauntecleer: no doubt if he could speak he would feel that our amusement at his predicament is unkind; but our feelings are detached rather than antipathetic. We feel no urgent sympathetic concern.

If, however, Geoffrey of Vinsauf could testify he would certainly be annoyed. He would have no doubt of the derision in our attitude towards him.

The passage I have quoted must also be seen in relationship to the general unfolding of the tale. It is part of a longer passage of triple invocation which deliberately holds the action up just after Chauntecleer has been snatched away by the fox. Although the narrative suspension is not strictly part of the literary humour it must be mentioned because the inactive quality of the passage is in comic contrast with the action that has just been set in motion. The passage builds up suspense, which is released by the sudden spurt of action when the narrative is resumed and the crowd is described rushing pell-mell after the fox. The full effectiveness of the passage I have quoted cannot be understood if it is taken in isolation from the rest of the poem.

One last point: the reference to Geoffrey of Vinsauf has often been taken as showing Chaucer's complete emancipation from the toils of rhetoric. Certainly, Chaucer can regard the master critically; but unless some feeling of respect were left, there could be no humour. From Geoffrey's point of view, no doubt the classical, derisive quality of the humour would be more in evidence. But from our point of view, on Chaucer's side, we may put in a plea for the English claim for kindliness in humour. Geoffrey is still treated with much respect: ' deere mayster soverayn ' are the harshest words that are said of him and who, knowing Chaucer's work, can think them totally in-

sincere? Geoffrey himself, could he know, might reflect
that through this reference his name is far more widely
known, and even respected, than it could otherwise have
been. He might also reflect, more ruefully, that
Chaucer shows himself still a devoted pupil. The
whole *Nun's Priest's Tale* is very rhetorical : the invocation to Geoffrey is in the best rhetorical tradition.
Even the mockery follows Geoffrey's own prescription :
if you wish to mock, he says in the *Nova Poetria* (ll. 431–
4), praise, but praise ridiculously : let your praise have
teeth.

It is clear that at least part of Chaucer's audience
was expected by him to have had a good general school-
ing in Latin and French literature, and to have a very
quick and sophisticated literary taste. Both he and
they felt strongly about literature. Questions of literary taste, however, often merged naturally into more
important questions concerned with morals and social
distinctions.

Such distinctions do not arise in *The Nun's Priest's
Tale*, but the implicit satire on the old tail-rhyme
romances and on old-fashioned English poetic diction
in general in *The Miller's Tale* is associated so closely
with humour arising out of class-distinctions, that it is
difficult to distinguish between them. There is a
very good example at the end of the description of
Alison.

> She was a prymerole, a piggesnye,
> For any lord to leggen in his bedde,
> Or yet for any good yeman to wedde.
>
> (I (A), 3268–70)

While this does full justice to Alison's charms, it is obviously a joke which lords were more likely to appreciate than were yeomen. Yet it is not satirical towards yeomen. It simply accepts them as a lower order of society. The unity on which the comic contrast between lord and yeoman rests is the potential male sexual relation to Alison. The contrast is of course that between illicit sexual relations and marriage. The joke here is based on our strong and naturally ambivalent feelings about sex and class, and here, moreover, there is a further contrast between sex and class : equality in sexual desire, inequality in class response.

The consciousness of different class-levels in *The Miller's Tale* and to a lesser extent in *Sir Thopas* is found in another form in *The General Prologue*. What has already been said about Chaucer's class-feeling applies here very clearly. The only characters in *The General Prologue* who are portrayed without mocking humour are those who conform to the medieval ideal of society, that is, the Knight and Squire ; the Clerk and Parson (representing the two chief aspects of clergy, i.e. learning and the care of souls) ; the Yeoman of the Knight, and the Ploughman. There is nothing comic in any of these portrayals.* Each is content with his

---

* I have had pupils in Japan who think that the line which describes the Knight's behaviour as being ' as meeke as is a mayde ' (l. 69), is very funny. This is a good example of how cultural conventions affect our thought, and in this case, our understanding of humour. The line is not, of course, meant by Chaucer to be funny. It is part of the Knight's perfection, as it was of Malory's Sir Launcelot, to be bold as a lion in the field, and meek as a lamb in the hall,

place in society, and each does his duty within it to the
very best of his ability, without any evasion of responsibilities and obligations. All the other characters, with
the exception of the Host and Chaucer himself (neither
of whom are fully portrayed), are guilty of evading to
some degree their responsibilities and obligations.

Chaucer clearly associated himself with the ideal
framework of society, and within that framework he
associated himself with the knightly class. He does
not satirise the representatives of any class he could
recognise. This is interesting in a man who was so
obviously acutely conscious of incongruity. There were
plenty of grounds for him to satirise those who outwardly conformed to his ideal of society. The court
of Richard II offered abounding examples of incongruity
between knightly ideals and knightly practices, and it
would not have been dangerous for Chaucer to satirise
some of them, especially if they were in a different court-

as we find in the lament for Launcelot, *The Death of Arthur*, ed. E.
Vinaver, 1955. The tradition of Christian bravery is found as early
as the praise of the dead hero Beowulf, ' the kindest and gentlest of
men (*Beowulf*, l. 3182). The combination of bravery and gentleness is part of the ideal of ' the gentleman ' so powerful in English
up almost to the present day. It is still not impossible, as Mr.
Coghill once reminded me, to find English gentlemen, both brave
soldiers and devout Christians, who might have stood in essence for
the portrait of the Knight. At first sight there may seem to be a
comic incongruity between the fierceness of the Knight in battle and
his gentleness and modesty at all other times. But greater knowledge
of the tradition and of the complexities of human nature would
surely show that in fact there is nothing incongruous, and hence
nothing comic, in the combination of qualities. Each is appropriate
in its different circumstance.

faction. There were equally disparities between the Parson and Ploughman whom he portrays and those in real life, as we could guess from what is said in the descriptions themselves, and as everybody had been fearfully reminded in the violent Peasants' Revolt of 1381. We cannot suppose he was blind to these incongruities in knight and peasant, yet he does not draw satirical pictures of either. They fitted in, they represented the framework of society he approved of, which he was ' inside of ', and about which he had no ambivalent feelings.

The people he satirised were all those who evaded the ideal class-system, in an obvious social way, like the Man of Law, or who evaded the religious ideal like most of the clerics. Those who were not knights inevitably seemed lower than the knightly class, for if they had been knights they would not have been outside the system; and the knights were highest in the system. The Man of Law is a good example. In actual life he was socially at least the equal of Chaucer, whether or not he was drawn from a known person, Thomas Pinchbeck, whom Chaucer had no reason to love. But he is open to satire, as a knight would not have been. And because the theory was idealistic and didactic it seemed natural that those who did not fit in could be expected to break the laws of society largely designed to support the class-theory and keep everyone in his place. It was rather simpler with the clerics. The religious ideal was so clear and well-known, the abuses so open, the tradition of anti-clerical satire so well-established, that it is not surprising to find them satirised.

No one in the fourteenth century could say a good word for the friars except the friars themselves.

The comic contrast, then, in the comic characters of the *Prologue* is based primarily on the clash between the ideal and the real. The clash was originally the more vivid because undoubtedly many of the portraits represented real people, known to, and in at least some cases disliked by, the members of Chaucer's own immediate circle; the humour of caricature was added to the other kinds of humour.

Of direct class feeling about the status of particular persons, as opposed to the more general feeling arising from the ideal class theory, there is not much in *The General Prologue*. The characters who seem to arouse it most clearly are the Prioress, the Tradesmen, and the Wife of Bath. Each is an example of that well-known English sport, climbing up the social ladder. The Prioress counterfeits courtly behaviour; the Tradesmen dress above their station, and their wives in particular, are socially ambitious; like them, the Wife of Bath is touchy about her social primacy and prestige in her parish. Social ambition in women is another typically English convention in both life and literature. The comedy arises from the incongruity between achievements or qualifications, and pretensions. (This type of the comic is also important in *The Reeve's Tale*, and is an element in *The Shipman's Tale*.) The natural feelings aroused are sympathy and contempt (in varying degrees), if we are already well superior to the social climber; sympathy and rage if we are her equal, and feel we may be outdone. Chaucer's humour is as usual of the superior kind.

The comedy of social pretension merges into another sort which is more frequent in *The General Prologue* and elsewhere; the comedy of what I have called ' hypocrisy '. By ' hypocrisy ' I mean the ordinary sense of the word, ' pretending to be good when one is bad ', but I wish also to include in the word all the deceptions revealed in the characters, from the comparatively innocent and almost unconscious deceptions of the prioress, to the financial dishonesty of Shipman, Miller, Reeve and Manciple, and on to the much greater dishonesty and deceit of Friar, Summoner and Pardoner, which involve an exploitation of the poor and innocent that enraged Chaucer. It would take too long to look at every simple example of ' hypocrisy '. The comic incongruity is in general the conflict between pretension and actuality, and our response varies between sympathy, liking, admiration for ingenuity, etc. on the one hand, and on the other various kinds of contempt. The resultant emotions vary very much. The Prioress is absurd, but we do not feel that she is very bad. Our amusement though superior is sympathetic. A more complex set of feelings is aroused by the Monk. Chaucer treats him ironically, but perhaps Chaucer's own feeling towards him was not quite resolved, and Chaucer really did admire without check his business ability. At the end of the scale of feeling the Pardoner is treated with savage humour. The Pardoner is comical, but the humour is one of disgust. Comic incongruity arises out of the Pardoner's physical qualities, out of the forged relics he carries, and out

of the profit he makes from the poor and innocent, all
based on the difference between what he is and what
he pretends to be. Brilliant as the portrait is, it is not
one of the great masterpieces of Chaucer's humour as
such, because the antipathy of feeling is so little checked
by sympathy, admiration, pity, or even understanding.
Chaucer's toleration had strict limits. Lacking, like
all men of his time, any historical view of the individual,
as of society, he had no conception that a man is what
he is largely because he has been made what he is.
The verse of A. E.'s that Mr. Grahame Greene is so
fond of,

> In the lost boyhood of Judas
> Christ was betrayed,

with its call on our pity and understanding even for
the wicked, would have meant nothing to Chaucer.
Chaucer therby avoided the source of some sentimentality, but he also lacked a source of deep understanding
of men.

The Pardoner's hypocrisy is explored more fully in
the wonderful *Prologue to the Pardoner's Tale*, which is
itself an interesting device for the comic revelation of
hypocrisy. The *Prologue* is a confession, completely
unashamed, of all the Pardoner's tricks and vices :

> What, trowe ye, that whiles I may preche,
> And wynne gold and silver for I teche,
> That I wol lyve in poverte wilfully?
> Nay, nay, I thoughte it nevere, trewely !
> For I wol preche and begge in sondry landes ;
> I wol nat do no labour with myne handes,

> Ne make baskettes, and lyve therby,
> By cause I wol nat beggen ydelly.
> I wol have moneie, wolle, chese, and whete,
> Al were it yeven of the povereste page,
> Or of the povereste wydwe in a village,
> Al sholde hir children sterve for famyne.
> Nay, I wol drynke licour of the vyne,
> And have a joly wenche in every toun.
>
> (VI (C), 439–53)

Some critics raise all sorts of problems for themselves by taking this speech completely literally, as if it were a speech out of a nineteenth-century play. The confession is psychologically improbable, at the very least, and in the supposed circumstances of the pilgrimage quite incredible. It was not intended to be realistic, and its lack of realism is the source of its comic quality. The incongruity arises from putting into the mouth of a villain a true account of his villainy such as he would never himself confess. The account is thus both true and untrue, and in each case highly discreditable. This device for exposing villainy is far more effective than straightforward accusation. In this piece substitute ' he ' for ' I ', ' him ' for ' me ', etc., and the piece loses all its comedy and piquancy. When the Pardoner speaks his own villainy, the conflict of feelings is between sympathy (inevitable when we read or hear what is supposed to be personal) and extreme antipathy for his ruthless treacherous selfishness. The incongruity of self-exposure is based on apprehension of the villainies, set against the joy and relief that they are made harmless by being revealed.

Self-revelation by a villain is first found, so far as I
know, in the long confession of Faux-Semblant in *Le
Roman de la Rose*, but it continues in the drama at least
as late as Shakespeare. At the beginning of *Richard
III*, Gloucester says, ' I am determined to prove a
villain ', and perhaps there is something inherently
comic in this simple device, for it is rare not to hear an
audience laugh at the statement. Most actors give
even the similar confessions of Iago and Edmund a
certain roguish, knowing, jovial air which it is hard to
believe Shakespeare intended, but which the device
lends itself to.

In Chaucer's treatment of the Pardoner especially,
but also in his treatment of many other characters,
humorous or serious, we are bound to be conscious of
a passionate if unassertive moral sense. He approves
of Knight, Clerk, Parson, Ploughman, for moral reasons :
he disapproves, or at any rate, makes mock of, most of
his other characters also for moral reasons. This
passionate moral sense, frequent in English literature,
is nearly always important in English humour. It is
strong in Chaucer, as in Shakespeare, Pope, Fielding,
Dickens, or the latest comic novels. The particular
flavour of much English humour derives from it, although the morals themselves may change. But a strong
moral sense alone does not provide a comic situation.
There must be a force opposed to it. This force is not
a secret enjoyment of, or desire for, immorality, whether
sexual, financial, or other, though no doubt there is
something in unregenerate human nature which does,
or would like to, rejoice in immorality. At least in

Chaucer, however, the force contrary to moral condemnation comes out in the form of enjoyment of the-thing-in-itself.   This is a quality difficult to illustrate textually :   it is best seen in such phrases as the Pardoner's,

Myne handes and my tonge goon so yerne
That it is joye to se my bisynesse.   (VI (C), 398–9)

This, with the simile that precedes it, suggests something of the simple pleasure that Chaucer finds in life and action of any kind.   It is a feeling strong in the Middle Ages, arising from the doctrine of ' plenitude ', by which it was held that God of necessity created all kinds of possible life, and all kinds of possible life had their place and value in ' the Great Chain of Being '.   There is a powerful life-delighting stream of thought in the Middle Ages that is too often unrecognised, and which found one of its greatest spokesmen in Chaucer.   So that even the Pardoner, especially because he is so efficient, is a spectacle we delight to see, even when going about his wicked and dishonest tricks.   Chaucer and through Chaucer we ourselves, delight in his quintessential ' Pardoner-ishness '.   A similar feeling of simple delight in what is created comes out in Chaucer's expression for the Monk, ' *a manly* man ', in *The Squire's Tale* the equivalent phrase, ' a horsly horse ' and in the *yemanly* of *The General Prologue* (l. 106): and phrases apart, the feeling is widespread in Chaucer.   It establishes a sense of absolute value and delight in life of any kind. And when this delight is yoked with moral disapprobation we get that peculiarly Chaucerian humour and satire which proceeds from strength, or detachment, not from weakness. Pope's satire often gives us the feeling, natural enough in his circumstances, that he has been hurt by life, and is consequently warped. Chaucer never gives us that feeling. He has an Olympian detachment. Some of this may derive from his sense of class superiority : but more of it comes from holding nothing absolutely contemptible : in the words of the common phrase of his time, that he also uses, ' God made nothing in vain '—not even a Pardoner. ·

This delight in God's creatures, mixed up with a very complex set of moral attitudes, is at the bottom of the last main subject of Chaucer's humour that I shall discuss : women.

Women in Chaucer's work are grouped socially like men for the purposes of humour. He never makes fun of upper-class women, except for the Prioress, who, as a cleric, falls into a special satire-attracting category. For upper class women he has only reverence. The only really lower-class poor woman of importance in Chaucer's poetry is Griselda, in *The Clerk's Tale*, and she too, like the Plowman, is an ideal (though not unreal or unconvincing) creation. The women who are comic, or take part in comedy, are those who correspond to what we might call nowadays the lower-middle class, wives who have to do housework, or have a single maid ; women whose husbands could never be called rich, but are not in danger of actual hardship and starvation, varying from carpenters to tradesmen and on to rather well-to-do merchants. It may be thought that an exception to the rule that only middle-class women are the subject of comedy is provided by the wife of the knight, January, in *The Merchant's Tale;* but she signally confirms it. When Placebo proposed her as a wife to January

He seyde ther was a mayden in the toun
Which that of beautee hadde greet renoun,
Al were it so she were of smal degree. (IV (E), 1623–5)

To be of small degree is to be of low rank : it is clear for several reasons that May was no lady, though she becomes one technically by her marriage to January.

One of the comic aspects of women is of course their desire to improve the station of life to ' which it has pleased God to call them '. This has been sufficiently suggested already, and is anyway a minor aspect.

The two major comic aspects of women are of course the sexual and the marital, and it is not easy to distinguish between the two. The sexual is perhaps the more fundamental. There is not much simple humour about sex in Chaucer. Needless to say he is never in the least pornographic, and is far less gross than Shakespeare. Social conventions of his time allowed him to describe certain physical functions and parts in short and plain words ; he makes infrequent use of this liberty, and the result when he does use it is, as one might have guessed, amusing but by no means dangerously exciting. However, Alison's sexual appeal, for example, is an obvious source of interest, and although it is not the chief source of the comic there can be little doubt that it helps to raise the emotional tension of the comic situation in *The Miller's Tale*. On the other hand, in the corresponding *Reeve's Tale* the chief

comic figure is the miller himself, and although the
sexual element adds to the interest of the tale, it is only
because sexual pride is the tenderest spot of both miller
and wife. In *The Merchant's Tale* the sexual antics of
May, and in *The Shipman's Tale* the sexual deceit of
the wife, contribute to the comic tension, but they are
not the main point of the comedy.

The chief example of Chaucer's humour about women
is in that extraordinary masterpiece, *The Wife of Bath's
Prologue*, one of Chaucer's greatest poems. Like *The
Pardoner's Prologue* it is a shameless confession of
vice : but it is much nearer to psychological possibility,
the vice is not felt to be so disgusting because it does
not prey on the poor and weak, and there is much more
balance in the comic contrasts. It is still not to be
taken realistically. The Wife's speech, for example, is
based on very wide reading of the anti-feminist literature
of the Middle Ages, and some critics have expended some
ingenuity in wondering how and when she could have
read such long and learned Latin treatises. Of course
she is not supposed to have done so. The Wife is not
to be supposed learned, any more than Macbeth is to
be supposed a poet, or an opera singer to be supposed,
from the point of view of the dramatic illusion, a
musician. The Wife's learning (and poetry), Macbeth's
poetic expression, the opera singer's music, are the
mediums in which they exist, and are created by the
author or composer. There is a special comic relationship, however, between the Wife and the material of her
speech. The Wife is a kind of feminist, yet her speech
is larded with extracts from the bitterest anti-feminist

satires.   She is herself the justification of nearly all that
men have said against women.   But just as there is a
sense of Chaucer's enjoyment in the spectacle of the
Pardoner even as he is, so there is an even more intense
feeling of joyful zestful life in the presentation of the
Wife.

> But Lord Crist! whan that it remembreth me
> Upon my yowthe, and on my jolitee,
> It tikleth me aboute myn herte roote.
> Unto this day it dooth myn herte boote
> That I have had my world as in my tyme.
>
> (III (D), 469–73)

We are bound to respond with sympathetic delight to
this joyous energy, and the fact that it is expressed in
such resolute unashamed gusto for sexual pleasure,
that universal human desire, makes our response the
richer.   The humour arises from the complication of
this response with others that are set against it.   In the
first hundred and fifty lines or so of *The Wife of Bath's
Prologue* there is a conflict between this sexual energy
and the demand for chastity.   We probably do not feel
the complication here so intensely as Chaucer did, because in the modern world most people feel less intensely
the spiritual sanctions that may be attached to chastity.
So we are less shocked, and consequently less amused, by
the Wife's ingenious and highly reasonable arguments
against chastity.   The essence of the comic conflict
here is to feel equally strongly on both sides of the
question, as it is highly likely both Chaucer and his
audience did.   We need not suppose that a strong
feeling about chastity implies lack of feeling about sex.

However, the main subject of the comedy in *The Wife of Bath's Prologue* is not sex but marriage. Marriage is a very fruitful subject for comedy : it appeals to strong interests and desires ; sexual, financial, social, and also, and especially, to interests and desires connected with status, with superiority and inferiority. The Middle Ages, with their hierarchical view of the universe and human society, and Chaucer himself, were particularlry interested in superiority and inferiority. Even apart from the strong natural interest, it is a good subject for comedy, because it is composed of two persons who in the fourteenth century were considered to be indissolubly linked. The persons provide a natural duality, and since they may easily be incongruous, the duality may easily become comic. Since they could hardly be divorced, the unity in incongruity which the comic demands was also present. The main incongruity in marriage was naturally the assertion of the wife's superiority over her husband, and the Wife most vigorously asserts hers. Throughout the *Prologue* we are shown other comic conflicts and incongruities within this general one : how she makes old husbands labour in love ; how she makes them at the same time give her valuable presents for her favours ; how she betrays them ; how she provides a new one against the death of the old, and so forth.

Our feelings are carried through a wide range of responses, pity, sympathy, disgust, for the husbands ; admiration, apprehension, vivid realisation and sympathy, strong dislike, for the Wife. Not the least of the pleasures in reading the *Prologue* is the witty distor-

tion of anti-feminist writing by the Wife, and the way
her use of such writing rebounds against her, just as
the Pardoner's cynical use of moral themes rebounds also
against him.   Another source of the comic, arising out
of the use of anti feminist writings, is the implied comparison of the Wife of Bath with other women of her
class really alive in the world.   She is a generalised image
of womankind as Alison in the *Miller's Tale* is not.

In so far as she slightly resembles any women of our
aquaintance we are amused ; she is a sort of distorting
mirror for women, a comically distorted image, which
yet has some true unity with the real nature of women.
The similarity and discrepancy causes amusement
which may have a greater or less satirical or hostile tinge.
She is also part of another implicit comparison and
contrast, of a somewhat similar kind.   She expresses a
natural reaction from the too-idealistic, medieval heroine.
The typical medieval heroine such as Emily in *The
Knight's Tale* inevitably calls for the Wife of Bath and
Alison of *The Miller's Tale* as compensations.   Criseyde
is fully woman, but alas she is also weak and treacherous.
Emily is too little sensual, the Wife too much.   But
since the ideal of woman was the Emily-type, the Wife,
so obviously and exactly opposite, gains as a humorous
and satiric creation.   She is opposite in every way :
lusty and desirous instead of remote and preferring
chastity ; realistic and contemporary instead of idealised
in an ancient setting ; married not virgin.   In every
respect she conflicts with the ideal ; she is satirised
for being so, and yet she is so life-like !

The same comic conflict between the ideal and an

exaggerated realism appears at the end of *The Clerk's Tale*, when after telling us of the superhuman goodness and incredible patience under incredible trials shown by the patient Griselda, the poet adds a mocking Envoy advising ordinary wives on no account to behave like Griselda in real life.

Here is a suitable opportunity to point out that just as Chaucer's comedy is always set in middle-class (not low) life; so Chaucer's comedy always uses realistic contemporary English settings and characters, in contrast to his serious poetry, which is always set in remote times and places. It is not true to say that the comedy is itself realistic. The comic plots themselves are more fantastic than the plots of the serious poems. There is nothing at all fantastic in *Troilus and Criseyde*, whereas nearly everything that happens in the comic tales is either fantastic, or fantastically ordered. Hence more comedy. We recognise the setting. The absurdity of the events contrasts with the familiarity, the concrete local quality of the setting. The contrast between strange events and the realistic setting is refreshing and stimulating; since it is also incongruous it is amusing as well.

VI

Humour and Poetry

The consideration of the chief comic subjects in Chaucer, inadequate as it has necessarily been, has already shown something of the structure of his comic imagination; his serene and rather detached superiority,

his orthodoxy, his moral sense and compassion. He is
the Insider, hostile to and amused by what is disorderly,
subversive, unorthodox. His humour is near to Bergson's concept of humour as a social corrective, except
that such is his pleasure in the varied forms of existence
that condemnation never seems to imply the wish either
to improve or punish.

Beneath all this is a special quality of mind and
feeling easier to illustrate than analyse : of his dream
recorded in *The House of Fame*, he says

> And whoso thorgh presumpcion,
> Or hate, or skorn, or thorgh envye,
> Dispit, or jape, or vilanye,
> Mysdeme hyt, pray I Jesus God
> That (dreme he barefot, dreme he shod),
> That every harm that any man
> Hath had, syth the world began,
> Befalle hym therof, or he sterve,
> And graunte he mote hit ful deserve.   (ll. 94–102)

In *The Parliament of Fowls*

> Yit that thow canst not do, yit mayst thow se
> For many a man that may nat stonde a pul,
> It liketh hym at the wrastlyng for to be.   (ll. 163–5)

When Troilus and Criseyde are at last brought together
in a long, rich scene of tender and innocent sensuality,
in the early part of which Troilus has swooned with
anxiety, he at long last finds courage when he knows
himself forgiven ; and then, Chaucer continues,

> This Troilus, with blisse of that supprised,
> Putte al in Goddes hand, as he that mente

Nothyng but wel; and sodeynly avysed,
He hire in armes faste to hym hente.
And Pandarus, with a ful good entente,
Leyde hym to slepe, and seyde, " If ye be wise,
Swouneth nought now, lest more folk arise ! "

(III, 1184–90)

And he makes Theseus in *The Knight's Tale* say, when
he finds Palamon and Arcite fighting so fiercely for the
love of Emily

But this is yet the beste game of alle,
That she for whom they han this jolitee
Kan hem therfore as muche thank as me.
She woot namoore of al this hoote fare
By God, than woot a cokkow or an hare !

(I (A), 1806–10)

These quotations, not drawn from the comic tales,
show the capacity of Chaucer's mind to relish and
respond to comic incongruity ; and they show too a
lightness of touch, a balance, a capacity to see around
a situation, to see the unexpected, to refresh the obvious
and relate it to a scheme of life ; in a word a delicate
simultaneous awareness of many different aspects of life,
which is of the essence of his sense of humour, as it is
not of the wilder, unhappier, more delirious, equally
great humour of Dickens. It is this sensibility which
also keeps his humour, with rare exceptions, under
control. His humour is not as impertinent to his serious
matter as some critics believe. And it is this same
sensibility which gives his humour its poetic quality.
Is there anyone who will deny the essentially poetic force
of humour ? If poetry's function is to detect ' the before

unapprehended relations of things ', surely that too is the function of humour. Humor is for ever putting things in fruitful relation to each other, comparing them, at the same time that it is revealing contradictions and contrasts. The process of comparison with a difference that is the essence of humour is the process of simile and even more, of metaphor, which is the fundamentally *literary* mode of experience, and one of our fundamental ways of thinking. Poetry arises out of metaphor, and equally surely, poetry (which is not necessarily written in verse) arises out of humour. And as poetry brings illumination to mind and heart, so does humour. The comparisons and contrasts intrinsic in humour illuminate in a new way old impressions ; the world is fresher, more stimulating, for the special illumination brought by humour. The world, too, may be seen in a truer light : the world may equally be comic as tragic. In Chaucer's humour, too, there is a sense of security. It is based on a sense of permanent and humane values, and an enviable belief in Providence. ' God makes nothing in vain.'

SHAKESPEARE

AND THE IMMORTALITY OF THE SOUL

It is possible to argue that tragedy and Christianity are incompatible. It is not possible to argue that Shakespeare was not a Christian. If he wrote tragedy at all, it was Christian tragedy. That does not mean that we need to be Christians to appreciate it, any more than we need to believe in Zeus to appreciate Homer. But we shall understand and enjoy Shakespeare better for understanding what he thought about the world; and understanding leads to critical conclusions.

The general culture in which Shakespeare lived was essentially the culture of medieval European Christianity. For all the changes in the sixteenth century, medieval European Christian thought and feeling was dominant in England. The Church of England preserved most of the services of the old medieval Church intact. Medieval sermons were still preached, sometimes from fifteenth-century manuscripts. Medieval romances were staple reading. ('What is Thisby' asks Flute the Bellowsmender, 'a wandering knight?') The chief English authors were Chaucer and Gower. Langland also was printed and read. Most of the printed books were medieval books. When an encyclopaedia was produced, it was 'Batman upon Bartholomew', i.e. Stephen Batman's edition of the English translation made by Trevisa at the end of the *fourteenth* century of the famous *thirteenth-century* Latin encyclopaedia of Bartholomaeus Anglicus. The most important book of the sixteenth century had been the most important book for centuries before; the Bible. More Englishmen read it; they read it in a more literal and less sophisticated way, but there was no fundamental change of attitude. When men read the classics Ovid was still, as for centuries before, the favourite author. Chaucer and Shakespeare are our great English Ovidians, though Milton in youth ran them close. Greek studies did not affect the imagination, as far as one can see, even of Ben Jonson. This is why the old-fashioned view of ' the Renaissance ', still prevalent in Japan, is so misleading. It would be possible to illustrate the medieval quality of Shakespeare's thought and feeling in many different ways. Take almost any point of any play at random and you can detect some medieval quality. It would be possible to argue that Shakespeare is the finest flower of English medieval culture.

To emphasise Shakespeare's medieval quality is not, however, to assert that he felt and thought just like a man of the earlier centuries. The earlier centuries differed sharply from each other, the fourteenth from the fifteenth, and naturally the sixteenth differs from both. But there is a closer organic similarity between Shakespeare's attitude to life and that of preceding centuries, than there is between Shakespeare's attitude and later centuries. The greatest change starts towards the end of the eighteenth, but it is clear that even by Dryden's time much of the medieval tradition found in Shakespeare was misunderstood, even though Dryden could still appreciate Chaucer. For, needless to say, medieval culture in England was already being undermined in the sixteenth century ; it was already doomed.

This, however, is too large a subject for the present essay. I propose to discuss one aspect of Shakespearian tragedy in the light of Shakespeare's mainly medieval suppositions about the nature of the universe, especially as they affect one doctrine, one aspect of the imagination; that is, the belief in the immortality of the soul.

First, a word about Shakespeare's personal beliefs. Some critics consider him to have been profoundly unchristian (and of course they mean it as a compliment !). The only way to defend this assertion is by the further assertions that either Shakespeare was a deeply dissimulating hypocrite, or that he was extremely ignorant of the tendencies of his own deeper imagination. For it is obvious that Shakespeare was, at least superficially, a Christian. It can be proved historically, or by reference to the plays. Such proof is not of course proof of the truth of Christianity. In any case modern Christianity is far different, even in England, from sixteenth-century Christianity. We are not engaged in religious controversy or propaganda, but simply stating what one would have thought an obvious fact, when we say that Shakespeare was a normal, orthodox, convinced, conforming, sixteenth-century Christian member of the Church of England, as far as he or anyone else knew. Atheists in Elizabethan England were rare enough to be immediately noticed and disliked. Think of the fuss about Marlowe's and Raleigh's so-called atheism (which was apparently, like Shelley's, more a form of deism). No one made this fuss about Shakespeare, yet he was well-known in London, and moved at least on the fringe of courtly and hence governing circles. The usual automatic thing for people was to be Christian. They were fined if they didn't go to church. In Shakespeare's plays there are abounding casual reflections of Christian belief and a large number of Biblical reminiscences. Now and again positive and clear-cut expressions of contemporary Christian belief are found in the plays, and the moral quality of the characters is measured against them, most notably in *Measure for Measure* (Isabella) and *Macbeth* (the hero himself). Although such clear-cut expressions are put into the mouths of particular characters, good or bad, the sentiments they express are built into the whole structure of the play. There is moreover a powerful impersonal descriptive narrative element in all Shakespearean poetic drama— the kind of thing that makes characters describe their own selves, as well as, where necessary, the local scene. The sentiments expressed through the structure and the impersonal, narrative, descriptive quality of the verse are those that are accepted both by the audience and by the dramatist. They can only arise out of such cultural unity: and they are of course the normal, accepted, sixteenth-century, Christian conventions.

Of these conventions I shall discuss the concepts of dualism, order, sin, and immortality. It is important to recognise them, because many people today do not hold them, and Shakespeare did.

The most general concept is dualism. The word describes not a belief held by Shakespeare, but a more

or less unconscious attitude.   There are many different
kinds of dualism in English thought, and perhaps in
all human religious thought.   What I am concerned
with here is the dualism traced by A. O. Lovejoy in his
Great Chain of Being between what is sometimes called
' thisworldliness ' and ' otherworldliness ' ; that is, between love of the world, and contempt of the world.
From Plato to the eighteenth century or later Western
European philosophical thought has nourished two apparently contradictory attitudes to the world ; one, an
attitude which regarded the world as delightful in itself
and as the embodiment of divinely-created values and
beauty : the other, an attitude of contempt to the world,
regarding it as nothing in comparison with the glories
of the Ideal, or Real World, which is beyond the senses ;
or, in the Christian case, in comparison with Heaven.
Set against Heaven, the world may seem merely a dis-
traction, or a stumbling-block, or an abomination,
meriting only our neglect or contempt.   This dual
attitude of love and contempt, thisworldliness and other-
wordliness, originating chiefly in Greek philosophy,
united with Biblical Doctrine.   The Old Testament
states that God made the world, and saw that it was
good.   Since we can attribute nothing evil to God,
and since he is thought of as the Creator of the world,
what he has made must be good.   In the New Testament it is said that God himself so loved the world that
he gave his only-begotten Son to save it.   Here is
support for thisworldliness.   On the other hand, the
New Testament in especial re-iterates a thorough-
going contempt for the world.   When the rich young

man asked what he should do to be saved, he was told to sell all he had and give it to the poor. This at any rate looks like contempt for worldly goods and comfort. ' Love not the world ' says the first Epistle of John, ' neither the things that are in the world. If any man love the world, the love of the Father is not in him . . . And the world passeth away, and the love thereof; but he that doeth the will of God abideth for ever.' Here is support for otherworldliness.

The New Testament's otherworldliness agreed particularly well with much in the philosophical and moral writing of the last period of the classical Latin world, especially with the teachings of Stoicism. It is safe to say that with this theoretical impulse, and helped by the actual course of history, and by whatever degree of truth the concept holds, Contempt of the World was the dominant attitude in the theory of life throughout the Dark and Middle Ages. There were a number of treatises with the very name, *De Contemptu Mundi*, one of which Chaucer translated in a lost work. The otherworldly attitude survives in Shakespeare in his Friars, in Lear's and Prospero's plans for retirement, and elsewhere.

But no human being, or human society, can fully hold to a doctrine of otherworldliness, and continue to live. It is of the essence of the human situation that both Contempt and Love of the World co-existed, even though otherworldliness might be dominant.

Thisworldliness does not emerge as an important force in Christian thought until the twelfth century. Times were too hard for it before. In the twelfth century,

the famous School of Chartres began to assert the
goodness of the world, as had not been done before.
The implications of the doctrine of divine creation
began to be felt. The visible universe began to be
looked upon with favour not only for its beauty but as
a manifestation of divine law and goodness. Existence
could therefore be thought of more enthusiastically as
a good: as Hamlet says 'conception is a blessing'.
And hence to take pleasure in the world was legitimate.
Augustine in the fifth century, for example, not only
regards conception as sinful (though necessary) but
regards sexual pleasure as a mark of sin. Aquinas in
the thirteenth century so far differs as to consider that
sexual pleasures in Paradise would have been, were it
not for Adam's fall, even more intense than they are
now. I do not want to exaggerate the difference between the two saintly doctors. Augustine was not a
gloomy kill-joy nor Aquinas a jolly old Pandarus.
Nevertheless there is here, as elsewhere between Augustine and Aquinas, a development that was also a
change. Aquinas shows a much more subtle view of
the world, and allows a far more dualistic attitude to it,
perhaps to the detriment of his philosophy (as Lovejoy
suggests) but hardly to his good sense. In Aquinas,
in the views he represents and makes possible at his
time and after, there is much more room for legitimate
delight in the world.

What this means in English literature can be partly
illustrated from Chaucer's great poem, *Troilus and
Criseyde*, not that Chaucer had read Aquinas, but because he was in some ways a representative man of his

times. For almost the whole of the poem the story of
Troilus's love affair is told in 'thisworldly' terms.
The hero is not immoral, nor is he an atheist, nor is
he always happy: but his story is set in a world where
delight is possible and legitimate, even if not continuous,
and where there is a strong sense of moral order and
moral law, even when that law is broken. When the
hero's love affair goes wrong and he dies, we feel the
pity and loss of a tragedy of waste and misfortune, like
that of *Romeo and Juliet*. But the hero is of course
immortal. When he dies, he enters the afterlife, the
other-world, and he laughs at all the trouble of this
world. This epilogue makes modern readers uncomfortable. It seems that all the sympathetic suffering we have endured for Troilus has been wasted. The
discomfort is caused partly because we tend not to read
with the detachment we should. Chaucer did not expect his readers to identify themselves with a passionate
young man, who, however noble and brave he was, was
also a little foolish. The chief cause of our discomfort,
however, is our lack of capacity to imagine the afterlife as vividly as Chaucer could, so that we are, paradoxi-
cally, more vividly aware of the differences between
this world and the other world. In consequence there
seems too great a gap of feeling between the body of
the poem and the epilogue; we may feel that Chaucer
ought to have made us aware of what we may call in
Mr. Greene's phrase, this 'fourth dimension , earlier
in the poem. Of course Chaucer assumes this awareness in us: but the actual conduct of the poem may
perhaps be blamed for its lack of suggestion of the

' fourth dimension ' of immortality.   Certainly, until
we come to the epilogue we are very strongly conscious
of Chaucer's apparently exclusive thisworldliness.
(There is of course no suggestion that thisworldliness
is necessarily pagan or atheist : far from it.)

In the fifteenth and sixteenth centuries, as W. E.
Farnham has so well shown in *The Medieval Heritage of
Elizabethan Tragedy*, thisworldliness steadily increases.
To cut a long story short, by the end of the sixteenth
century practically everyone was agreed that it was
legitimate to take pleasure in the world ; that the world
had an inherent moral order ; and that God's omnipo-
tence and omniscience lay over it.   There is nothing
here that Aquinas would have disagreed with in the
thirteenth century.   Indeed, the classic English statement of the divinely-ordained law and order of the world
is Book I of Richard Hooker's *The Laws of Ecclesiastical
Polity*, which directly derives (with modifications of
course) from Aquinas.   Only the balance is different.
In earlier centuries the seesaw was heavily weighted on
the side of Otherworldliness.   Gradually there was less
contempt and more love of the world expressible in men's
imaginations.   At some period in England between
Chaucer and Shakespeare's time the seesaw was level.
Slowly it began to tilt downwards towards the side of
thisworldliness.   Puritan thought (and its modern deri-
vants) is strongly thisworldly, (contrary to popular impression), and the Puritan revolution hastened the trend.
Nowadays, contempt is nowhere, or hides away in a
corner, love everywhere.   We are all thisworldly.   But
in Shakespeare, who was rather old-fashioned in thought,

(more medieval, for example, than many of his contemporaries), there is still a noticeable strain of otherworldliness.

In one respect, however, Shakespeare like all Elizabethans was entirely ' thisworldly ' ; that is, in his belief in the divinely-ordained order of the universe. Thanks to such works as Dr. Tillyard's *The Elizabethan World Picture* most readers are now well aware of the all-embracing scope of this concept of order, divine, human, and material, so important for our understanding of Shakespearean comedy and history, as well as tragedy. If we fail to recognise the importance of divine order in the world in Shakespeare's works, we may as well give up reading him and take cookery lessons on television.

A necessary part of the Elizabethan concept of order was the belief that any man was capable of recognising and abiding by that order. Here, as Farnham points out, is one of the fundamental differences between Elizabethan and Greek tragedy. In Greek tragedy a man may break a law which is not clearly established ; or he may be caught, like Orestes, between two contradictory but nevertheless divinely ordained laws ; and for breaking the law he is punished. Greek tragedy is highly religious, but the conventions are very different. In Shakespearean tragedy, with the possible exception of Hamlet, to be discussed later, man is not so cruelly victimised.

The difference between Greek and Elizabethan tragedy is partly due to the Elizabethan concept of sin, which is related to the earlier concept of the goodness of God and of creation. If God and the world are essentially good, how is it that the world is as we see it, full of imperfection and evil and suffering? The sixteenth century, like all the preceding medieval centuries, explained it by man's own exercise of free-will, choosing evil rather than good. Man alone of all God's creatures in the world, from stocks and stones upwards, had rebelled against God's law. And since he was chief of the creatures of the earth, his defection had stained creation everywhere. The fault for the world's imperfections lay not with God but with man.

The Elizabethan and Shakespearean view of divine order, and of evil in the world, demanded the Elizabethan and Shakespearean view of sin. The sense of sin, I am told, is lacking in the ancient Greeks and also in many Eastern peoples. Freud has made sin seem a bit old-fashioned, even in the West, though not everyone would say that the West has given up sin. We do not therefore automatically understand Shakespeare's position here. A sense of sin implies moral support, by the sinner, of the authority which condemns him. It recognises moral obligation, and deplores the breaking of that obligation. Consequently it implies a divided set of feelings in the individual sinner, and disapproval or distrust of the self. With a sense of sin there will also usually be a desire to atone, to repair the breach. A sense of sin or at least of guilt, is very strong in some writers—the Wordsworth of *The Prelude*, the Coleridge of *The Ancient Mariner*, the Shakespeare of *Hamlet*, spring to mind. Hamlet suffers from a paralyzing sense of sin. It is typical of such cases that the obvious cause of the feeling seems either non-existent or trivial.

Freud might account for it by the Oedipus complex, but it does not seem to be only sexual.

These special cases apart, according to general Christian belief, all men, save one, were sinful. The effect of this belief is to make man responsible for his sufferings as never before. To put it with crude emphasis, Hamlet, Othello, Macbeth, Lear, are responsible for their own sufferings as Oedipus is not. This is not a theory about a tragic flaw, a theory of the ' mole in nature ' which is fatal to the hero through an unlucky set of circumstances. Something the hero has *done* has brought about the tragedy. Shakespearean heroes are sinners, as Oedipus is not. There is a difference between guilt and sin. Guilt is a legalistic concept, sin a moral one. Oedipus, we might say, is a guilty man : it is an English maxim that ignorance of the law is no defence for crime. But Shakespeare's heros are not so much guilty (though that may follow) as sinful.

If this were all, the Christian concept of sin would be intolerable. There were at least two important corollaries which lightened the load. One was that sin was outside as well as inside. The tradition always insisted on the external and objective reality of evil, as well as its subjective reality in the corrupted human will. To put it in terms of the myth of Adam and Eve (a myth which was believed to be historically true for long after the sixteenth century) there is Satan as well as Adam. In terms of Shakespearean tragedy, Hamlet, Othello, Macbeth, Lear, represent Adam ; Claudius, Iago, the Witches, Goneril and Regan, are of the Devil's Party and know it.   Thus although man is responsible for his own fate, he has, as Adam had, an excuse.   Though he deserves punishment, he deserves help.   This makes way for the other corollary to the belief in sin, the belief in the Redemption of sinners by Christ.   Sin, and the evils introduced by sin, need not have absolute dominion. This last point will turn out to have great and somewhat surprisingly neglected importance in Shakespeare's tragedy.

Among all the evils that sin brought with it, the greatest was felt to be death, the evil which summed up all other evils.   It was Adam's sin, said Milton, which brought death into the world and all our woe; as a nineteenth century rhyme for young ladies has it,

> When Adam fell he opened Hell
> And damned us all to death!

Of course there are apparent inconsistencies in a Christian view which regards death as the worst of evils, but those need not concern us now.   There is no doubt that for medieval men the idea of death had a supreme emotional value.   Thus all the medieval and sixteenth-century definitions of tragedy, from Boethius through Chaucer to Puttenham, put death as the culminating evil. Farnham has described death as peculiarly the concern of Gothic (i.e. medieval and Elizabethan) tragedy, in this respect greatly differing from Greek tragedy.   This particularly Gothic sense of the horror of death was played on increasingly in the latter Middle Ages in England, until with many writers, sermon writers not the least, it became a morbid obsession.   It gave

Elizabethan and Jacobean audiences many a good shudder.   Death is the vile conqueror, even more vile, even more powerful, than Tamburlane.   One of Webster's characters says ' On pain of death let no man name death to me : It is a word infinitely terrible.'   Shakespeare himself in his earlier plays frequently evokes the shudder.

Mention of death inevitably brings with it the consideration of whether there is something after death. We are bound to use a terminology based on time here, and anyway, the Elizabethans naturally tended to think of eternity as infinite extension in time.   The Elizabethans (and I continue to use the term loosely to include the earlier part of the seventeenth century) naturally, since they were Christians, believed in life after death. Moreover, they believed in it complete with judgment, reward and punishment.   Such a belief is essentially otherworldly.   Man was an immortal soul, destined to go to Heaven or Hell for eternity.   This is to say what everyone knows : but for various reasons this destiny is much less a part of the modern religious and hence literary imagination than of the sixteenth century's.   It is important that we should try at least to re-imagine this eternal destiny, if only to understand earlier literature, to say no more.   This belief in immortality in Shakespeare and his audience, obvious as it is, needs to be emphasised.   I know no modern critic who has commented on it, yet it is a fundamental element in the tragedies.   It was so much taken for granted that it receives only casual mention (like the equally fundamental belief in Order, for the most part).   The presence

of the belief cannot be disputed, and it constitutes a
strong element of otherworldliness. Hamlet's mother
says to him

> all that live must die,
> Passing through nature to eternity.

In a scene where, because of forgetfulness of the apparently obvious fact of the belief in eternity, Hamlet's
motives are often misconstrued, Hamlet refuses to kill
the king when he is praying, because he thinks he would
be sending the king to heaven. The point of Hamlet's
famous soliloquy on suicide is the fear of something
after death, not the more characteristically modern fear
of annihilation.

In *Othello*, when Othello at last recognizes his crime
against Desdemona he says in one of his most pathetic
speeches,

> when we shall meet at compt [i.e. on the
>   Day of Judgment]
> This look of thine will hurl my soul from heaven
> And fiends will snatch at it.

In *Macbeth* the hero has deliberately ' jump'd the life
to come ' as he himself says, in favour of the here and
now, this bank and shoal of time. Macbeth himself
thus chooses to be purely thisworldly ; and see what it
brings him to. He knows well enough, and it makes
him desperate, that he has his

> eternal jewel [meaning his immortal soul]
> Given to the common enemy of man [meaning Satan].

In *Lear*, when Lear is dead, Kent expresses his own

sense of approaching death by saying he has a journey shortly to go,

> My master calls me, I must not say no.

We must beware of taking such remarks as mere figures of speech. They expressed literal truth for Shakespeare and his audience. Until the end of the nineteenth century (at least) the vast majority of Englishman held the same literal belief in personal immortality.

Nevertheless, while emphasising the force of this essentially otherworldly belief in Shakespeare and his audience, it will not do to over-estimate it. The emotional and imaginative force behind that belief had begun to wane in Europe at least from the fifteenth century. As the otherworldly trend of belief weakened, so did a present and vivid sense of the life after death. At the end of the sixteenth century it was still strong, but it was not dominant. What had become equally strong was a sense of the delightfulness of the world, a feeling for its moral order. There was, in a word, the possibility of a delicate balance, as I have already suggested, between thisworldliness and otherworldliness. A number of people achieved this balance in some measure in their lives and writings. But none achieved it so successfully as Shakespeare.

If we look at the tragedies with these concepts of the dualism of thisworldliness and otherworldliness; the moral order of the universe; mankind's sin and responsibility; and the immortality of the soul; we shall be able to understand some of the reasons for the unique achievement of Shakespearean tragedy.

First, it is clearly impossible to have tragedy at all without a strong thisworldly feeling, an intense delight in the world. If this did not exist, if the world is entirely to be despised, then suffering in it is only natural, and the sooner we are out of it, the better. And furthermore, some sense of moral order in the universe is necessary before we can have a sense of tragedy : for however we may define tragedy, it must show suffering where there could have been delight, and must show that something has gone wrong which could have, indeed ought to have, gone right. What has gone wrong in Shakespeare's tragedies is the moral order, with which is linked the material, social, spiritual, order of the world.

Moral judgments, or the consideration of moral questions, are not inherently necessary in the understanding of all literature. The moral quality is not the only quality of Shakespearean tragedy, nor perhaps the greatest. But it was important in the kind of literature people wrote and expected to read and hear in Shakespeare's time, and is much more important in Shakespeare than recent criticism, with some exceptions, has cared to admit. If Elizabethan literature is literature concerned with morality we cannot afford to neglect moral questions, any more than we can afford to neglect love in love-poems, nature in nature-poetry, war in war-poetry. And there can be no doubt, as older critics took for granted, and as now needs re-emphasis, that Shakespearean tragedy is concerned with moral evil. It is moral evil, and wicked men and women, which bring about the great tragedies, as is not the case with *Romeo and Juliet*. The ancestor, so to speak, of Shakespearean tragedy is *Richard III*. The moral evil is within the hero as well as without, less clearly in *Hamlet*, the earliest of the great tragedies, but clearly enough indicated by the nature of Hamlet's own reproaches—' I am myself indifferent honest, but yet I could accuse me of such things it were better my mother had not born me '. As to the other tragedies, the presence and importance of moral evil within and without the central hero needs no illustration.

From the thisworldly feeling for the delight and beauty and order that are naturally in the world, and from the contemplation of the sin and evil forces which destroy the joy and beauty and order, come the very possibility of tragedy. Tragedy is a matter for this world. When Chaucer suddenly takes up, without sufficient warning, an otherworldly attitude at the end of *Troilus and Criseyde*, he calls into question all our expense of sympathetic joy and suffering in the rest of the poem. If Shakespeare had done the same sort of thing, how could we possibly feel as we do in *Hamlet?* What if there were a final scene in which we actually saw the flights of angels carrying Hamlet to his rest, with Hamlet laughing at the foolish misery that he had endured on earth? That is the kind of thing Chaucer has done. One of the reasons why some critics say that Shakespeare was not fundamentally a Christian is because they consider a Christian was, and is, bound to do the same kind of thing that Chaucer does : Shakespeare *seems* entirely of this world in the ending of his tragedies.

Without a thisworldly delight in life there can be no

tragedy. And the stronger the delight in this life, the worse death may seem. The crown of tragedy, a crown of thorns, is the death of the hero. Shakespeare seems certainly to follow this pattern. All his tragic heroes die; and in contemporary definitions of tragedy, and in the plays of Shakespeare's contemporaries, in Gothic tragedy generally, death is the culminating woe. But in fact, no one surely feels in the four great tragedies, or in *Antony and Cleopatra*, that the death of the hero is truly a major part of the tragedy? In *Romeo and Juliet* death *is* the tragedy, but by general agreement that is a lesser work. In the great tragedies, death, we may say, is necessary: we cannot imagine the heroes living on (though Lear did all through the eighteenth century in Nahum Tate's version); but death is not important. Death is necessary to prevent anti-climax, and also as an act of mercy. With the possible exception of Hamlet, in a play which represents a transition from the normal convention to Shakespeare's own deeper tragic view, there is nothing left for the tragic hero to do but die: as Kent says of Lear, ' he hates him who on the rack of this rough world would stretch him longer.' Death is the least part of the suffering of the tragic hero, even of Hamlet.

At the end of the play it is no loss for the hero to leave the world, whether he be a sinner like Lear, who is purified and redeemed and worn out by his suffering, or a criminal like Macbeth, who has voluntarily damned himself and deprived his own life of all significance. And here we must call to mind again the slight but specific references to the life after death. With Chaucer

the full and open, almost realistic, treatment of the
life after death takes away from the tragic effect.   Shakespeare's references are slight enough not to nullify the
effect of finality, and not to make the earlier suffering
seem pointless or trivial.   But Shakespeare's references
to the life after death do ease the burden of suffering
at the end of the play.   We are put in mind, in a vague
and shadowy way, of the ultimate justice, the ultimate
reasonableness of the universe.   Even Othello's pathetic
reference to the Day of Judgment has this effect.   It is
a reference to justice.   By a paradox this otherworldly
sense of justice and recompense and reward invoked from
beyond the grave *reinforces* the thisworldly delight in
the beauty and moral order within the created universe.
This paradox is seen most clearly in the fate of Macbeth.
He has deliberately sought the highest good this world
can offer him—' the sweet fruition of an earthly crown '
—and has broken the moral order whose only sanction
can come from otherworldliness ;   the result of his denial
of the other world is that this world becomes shockingly
bitter and senseless :

> Life's but a walking shadow, a poor player
> That struts and frets his hour upon the stage
> *And then is heard no more ;*   it is a tale
> Told by an idiot, full of sound and fury,
> Signifying nothing.

This is no more Shakespeare's real opinion than
Gloucester's

> As flies to wanton boys are we to the gods ;
> They kill us for their sport.

Gloucester comes to a better frame of mind ('You ever-gentle gods' he says later); Macbeth does not, and so his tragedy is that he has now come to think life is truly what he has made it for himself. No other tragic hero reduces himself to such stark insensibility. Macbeth's death affirms the ultimate justice and reasonableness of the universe, because Macbeth has become a dangerous evil animal, whom it is just and reasonable should die. Macbeth is a Hitler. Only with Macbeth is death significant, but even here not as part of his tragedy, but as part of the purification of the world which comes at the end of all four great tragedies. Death here becomes the instrument of justice.

We feel at the end of the tragedies a deep relief and a new hope, because evil has been purged away (though at the cost of great pain and loss), and the ultimate goodness and rationality of the universe even beyond death have been re-asserted and re-created. This is why there is not that real horror and bitterness in Shakespearean tragedy that there seems to me to be in some Greek tragedy (like the *Antigone*) and especially in the *Iliad*. For this relief and hope the concept of immortality is vital. There are absolute moral laws in the *Antigone*, but no eternal compensation for Antigone in obeying them. I do not assert here that Shakespeare's view of life was more true than Sophocles (who also shows deep religious concern, incidentally), but only that Shakespeare is different and more consoling.

The pattern of Shakespearean tragedy is a Christian pattern, though not necessarily a modern Christian pattern. The tragedies present us with the spectacle of a derangement of the moral order for which, in some sense, the hero is at least partially responsible.*

In each play we are shown waste and suffering, but at the end goodness triumphs. Evil having arisen, it is conquered by the good, although the struggle necessarily involves the suffering of the good, as we see it daily in our lives. This is essentially the pattern of life as understood by Englishmen in the medieval and sixteenth centuries. The world, naturally good, was spoilt by sin; the sin was Adam's, guilty himself, but tempted through Eve by Satan, that is by the principle of evil himself. But the world was redeemed, the evil neutralised, by the innocent suffering of the best man who ever lived, Christ. Shakespeare's tragedies are secular. The divine element does not enter actively into them, as it was considered to have done in Christ, who was also God. The suffering of the good is not the suffering of the divine. There is no Christ in the tragedies. But the pattern is the same. At the end of the tragedies we have a sense of redemption, just as, after the tragedy of the crucifixion, we have the knowledge of the redemption through the risen and immortal Christ. The risen Christ corresponds to the immortality of the soul in the tragedies.

The whole process means waste and pain, of course.

---

* *Hamlet*, probably the earliest of the great tragedies is an exception as regards the plot, but one could argue, on some psychoanalytical basis that Hamlet is to be associated with Claudius, hating unawares his brilliant and overbearing father, loving his mother too much. Yet another reason why he cannot kill Claudius —Claudius is a projection of himself.

One good has been destroyed—Hamlet's youth, Lear's age, Othello's marriage, Macbeth's nobility. Nothing can alter that. The historical process is not meaningless, and what is done is done. But it is possible to drive the evil back, and find another good. Man can be redeemed. The pattern is seen clearest in *Lear*, the most Christian of all the tragedies. For the good that is lost at the beginning we find a greater good at the end—a purified and loving Lear. Good has come out of evil. It is hard to say his suffering has been purposive, but at least it has had a good effect. Again, in a literal sense Cordelia's death has not of itself redeemed Lear. But Cordelia's goodness and purity are essential to the play, and to Lear's final purification, and Cordelia does die for Lear. The suffering of the young, innocent and best is as inevitable to Lear's redemption, as, more clearly, the sufferings of the young, innocent and good are to the redemption of the elder generation in *The Winter's Tale*, *Cymbeline*, and *The Tempest*.

We must not go to extremes. I do not suggest that Shakespeare's conscious aim in his tragedies was in any sense Christian propaganda. The tragedies are all different. But they follow a pattern, and achieve a kind of effect, which can only be accounted for by the Christian pattern of thought of Shakespeare. We do not need to share his religious beliefs, any more than we need to share those of Sophocles, to respond to his tragedies. But in each case, sympathetic knowledge and understanding of the poet's beliefs quickens our responses. And in each poet there is, we must feel, a seed of reality set in the fruitful soil of conventional belief.

ASPECTS OF NATURE AND WORDSWORTH

I

The European Nature

The word 'nature' has represented many different ideas about the world, and about man. But in English literary use since the eighteenth century it has very frequently been used to mean 'natural scenery'. Very often, especially in the eighteenth century, ideas about 'the nature of the universe' have been mediated through the concept of natural scenery: so that very inconsistent meanings may be bundled up in the word. This is natural enough. Sight is the most vivid of the senses, and for us who are not philosophers, it is easy enough to confuse what we think and feel with what we see. Up to the nineteenth century the works of man occupied a smaller place in the world than what was 'naturally' there, and which was conceived to be the work of God. When man thought about the nature of the external universe he naturally thought about what he could see which was neither man, nor made by man. This was Nature, i.e. natural scenery, which was the world made by God, and was therefore the 'nature of the universe'. It is in this common meaning of the word, 'natural scenery', with more or less vague and muddled scientific and metaphysical implications within it, that I shall use the word 'Nature'.

The tendency of European literature until the twentieth century was to take the word as an absolute, as if Nature were everywhere fundamentally the same. That illusion has been destroyed by travel. The works of Mr. E. M. Forster give a good example. His first four novels treat Nature in the old European sense; a power for good, a beauty, a truth, even though sometimes terrifying and apparently cruel. His last novel, set in India, sees Nature as something much different; no longer a creative source of good, but either hostile or indifferent to man, cruel, often ugly, and equally a creature. Outside Europe the old concept of Nature will not do. The squalid fertility of the Tropics, the dusty or icy wastes of Australia or the Poles, the vastness of the American continent, all deny it. Even in Japan, lying mostly in a temperate zone somewhat similar to Europe's the old European idea of Nature will not do. Leaving aside the more terrible visitations of flood and typhoon, volcano and earthquake, the very countryside is different in form and feeling. What strikes an Englishman in Japan is the billiard-table flatness of the cultivated fields and the sudden steepness with which the mountains, shaggy with trees, stand abruptly out of the plain. The mountains are almost totally resistant to man; the small fields with their straight dikes and precise green lines of rice, every blade of which has been tended by hand, where there are no hedges, and hardly an inch of untouched space, are entirely subdued by man to his use. You cannot go on a country walk through the farming lands; a flooded paddy-field gives no opportunity for contemplation; you must pick your way. There are however plenty of places for contemplation and religious retreat, hallowed by long tradition : they are in the jagged mountains, unsmoothed by glacial or human action, covered with forest. Here were the essential homes of the Shinto deities, the retreats of Buddhist monks and hermits. In Japan neither the sown nor the wild is pastoral.

In England especially, Nature is neither so completely subdued nor so completely alien as it is in Japan. A field of wheat has its hedges. Crofts, or at least sheep with their shepherd, climb high up the modest sublimities of the mountains of Cumberland and the Pennines. Nature is seen almost everywhere in relation to the daily activities of men ; it is nowhere completely alien and dominant, nowhere, except in the industrial cities of the nineteenth century, completely crushed. Gradation and modification are in England of the essence of Nature ; her fierceness stops short of typhoon and volcanic eruption, yet her power is not completely tamed in the best-trimmed hedge or smallest suburban garden.

It was not always so. When the fierce fair-haired Anglo-Saxons first cut into the forests to make their villages they cannot have felt much confidence in the healing power of Nature. In *Beowulf* the man-eating monster Grendel typifies the spirit of the waste moorlands, the fen fastnesses where he has his home. From these places he is always liable to descend with cruel greed. It was just to such places that men in the nineteenth century turned for spiritual refreshment. In the eighth they were gloomy and dreadful to men. In the eighteenth and nineteenth centuries, the Lake District became a famous resort for those in search of the beauties of Nature, but the lake in *Beowulf* is the home of Grendel's mother, worse than Grendel, and the frost-rimed wood that hangs over it is sinister and deadly ;

> every night horrible marvels can be seen there, fire on the water ; therefore no wise man likes to look in its depths. Though the stag, the hart strong with horns, tormented by the hounds and pursued from far should come to that wood, he would die first on the shore, the princely crea-ture, before he would hide his head in the wood. It is not a pleasant place. When the wind blows, the hateful storm, the turmoil of the waves rises up dark to the sky, the air goes black, the heavens weep.
>
> (*Beowulf*, 1365–76, freely translated.)

There is no reason to think that such a place was notably ugly by our standards. Men brought different ap-prehensions, different eyes to it. Largely because of their inadequate physical command over Nature, Nature was a Grendel to the Anglo-Saxons—it was after them.

It is cultivation, but only a certain amount of cultiva-tion, that gives Nature the power to console, to teach, to heal ; that, and the creation of towns, which enables poets to live in the comfort of towns, experience their drawbacks, and contrast the town with the half-tamed Nature that makes ' the country '. ' God makes the country and man makes the town ', as was said in effect by Varro (*De Re Rustica*, III, I) in the first century B. C. In parts of Italy, especially in Rome, these two con-ditions, a partly-tamed countryside, and a contrasting,

entirely man-made town, had arisen by the first century
B.C. and influenced poetry. The balance was lost
when the barbarians came, and had to be painfully
striven for anew. It was in sight again in Europe
generally from the twelfth century onwards, and together
with developments in religion, philosophy and science,
in trade and social organization, made possible the
medieval idea of Nature.

It is often said that in Europe medieval men feared,
distrusted and condemned the natural world which was
perceived through senses which they believed to be
corrupt; and as in most wrong generalisations there is
some truth in this. But it is truer to say that medieval
men loved and revered Nature, if with awe, for they
thought of the world, spoilt as it was by man's delinquen-
cy, as the ordered and dutiful creation of Good. This
is well illustrated by a passage written about 1200 in
English in a life of St. Margaret. There is nothing
eccentric or unusual in the ideas expressed here; in
idea and expression the passage is the work of a minor
Hooker. This is the reality that lies behind the medieval
personification of Nature:

Invisible God . . . you made and control all worldly
things; those that exalt and praise you in heaven, and all
the creatures that dwell on earth; the fishes that float with
fins in the floods, the flying birds that fly in the air, and all
that is made, do what you wish and obey your laws,
except man alone. The sun runs her course without any
rest. The moon and the stars, who walk about the sky
neither cease nor stop, but move evermore, nor have
they ever turned aside anywhere from the way which

you have made for them.   You guide the ocean so that it
cannot flow further than you have marked.   The winds,
the weathers, the woods bow before you and obey.   Devils
and angels fear your wrath.   The creeping things and the
wild animals that live in this world live according to the
law that you have ordained for them, loving Lord.
> (*St. Margaret*, quoted *Early Middle English
> Texts*, ed. Dickins and Wilson, 1951, p. 97)

In the second half of the twelfth century a long process of hints and suggestions extending from Latin
antiquity culminated in the full personification of
Nature.   She appears first in the work of Bernardus
Sylvestris, and through the medium of the immensely
popular *De Planctu Naturae* of Alanus de Insulis this
personification of Nature spread to writers in the
European vernaculars.   In English she appears first in
Chaucer's *Parlement of Foules* and last in the Mutability
Cantos of Spenser's *Faerie Queen*.   Nature, for these
five medieval centuries, the twelfth to the early seventeenth, is a goddess, the deputy of God, in the form of
the most beautiful of women.   She personifies both
the concept of the constant creative force of God and
the concept of the order, beauty and essential goodness
of the created universe.   A feeling for natural scenery
does not play a large conscious part in this conception
of Nature.   But it is safe to say that such a conception
could not have arisen elsewhere than in Europe, and
within Europe, nowhere else than in the North of France,
the most developed part of Europe, the most civilised,
in the twelfth century, where town and cultivated
countryside were beginning to achieve a balance.   Ber-

nardus and Alanus are both writers of the 'School of Chartres', and as Mr. C. S. Lewis has shown in *The Allegory of Love*, both show an appreciation of the natural scenery of the countryside.

But in Chaucer's day the countryside of England was still very uncomfortable and dangerous in itself, and the resort of thieves and outlaws.   The nearest Chaucer and his contemporaries came to the later feeling for natural scenery, to that sense of relaxation and support, of the presence of some great beneficence, of

> a sense sublime
> Of something far more deeply interfused,
> Whose dwelling is the light of setting suns,
> And the round ocean and the living air,
> And the blue sky, and in the mind of man,
>   (Wordsworth, *Lines above Tintern*)

was in a garden or a walled park.   Literary convention apart, it is significant that when Nature appears in *The Parlement of Foules* she appears in a walled park with a double gate high enough for writing to appear at the top.   One could not imagine the goddess in the wilderness of the countryside.

Thus it is that the tradition of writing about Nature even in the sixteenth and seventeenth centuries, was largely confined to highly artificial pastoral poetry, set in 'Arcadia', of which the one sure thing is that it has as little to do with the English countryside as the sunny May dawns of Chaucer's poetry.   (Of course there are exceptions to the convention, but they are exceptions.)

It was first in the eighteenth century in England, with the growth of towns, and especially of the 'great wen'

of London; and with the rapid enclosure of the old
common-fields, and social developments that made
England comparatively safe to wander about in, that
Nature might become the kind of goddess who might
safely roam beyond the confines of the medieval park.
This is the process of the ' divinization of Nature ' that
Mr. Willey has described so well in *The Eighteenth
Century Background*, and which he considers began at the
Renaissance.   But Nature, as I have shown, was a goddess long before that.   For the first time, however, in the
eighteenth century, the general idea of Nature becomes
consciously associated in England with natural scenery;
thereby, in a very curious development, she becomes
also that very English figure, a lady schoolteacher;
stern, but with a softer side for her favourites :

> Let Nature be your teacher.
> > (Wordsworth, *The Tables Turned*)

II

Nature and History in the Eighteenth Century

Of the many aspects of Nature in the eighteenth century which have been noted, one has received less than
its due.   Nature in the eighteenth century, though only
in the eighteenth century, had History as an almost
inseparable companion, and the companionship, though
transient, has left an enduring mark.   History walks
hand in hand with Nature through most of the nature-
poetry of the century, and in very much of the poetry
of Wordsworth.

It is typical of the close association between Nature

and History that Gray, so often hailed as the precursor of Romantic feeling about natural scenery, should also be one of the first men in England to have a real feeling for ' the pastness of the past ', a real sense of its difference.   He was not absolutely without predecessors in the feeling either for Nature or for History.   Addison refers to the agreeable horror of mountains, while the first tourist of the antique in English literature is perhaps Sebastian in *Twelfth Night*, reflecting the interest of a number of young gentlemen travelling in Italy in the later sixteenth-century.   But Gray is typical of his century both in the strength of his two interests, and in uniting them : Nature and History for him are twins, and the one rarely appears in his writings without the other.   Much of the elegiac sweetness of the *Elegy in a Country Churchyard* derives from the mixture in the poem of the feeling for country life and the feeling for the past.   The feeling for the past is inherent in the very setting, a graveyard of an ancient church with its ' ivy-mantl'd tower '.   The church represents the very reason for the association, in England, of Nature with the evidences of the past.   Once you could wander about the country with any convenience, as you could for the first time in the eighteenth-century ; once, that is, that the countryside was tamed to the extent that natural scenery could be easily seen and reflected upon, almost every ' natural ' scene was found to have in it some evidence of England's past.   In rougher country there were either the ruined medieval castles that were once its guardians or its bane and terror, or there were the ruins of medieval monasteries which had sought the

wilderness because in the desolation men might be less
distracted in their search for God ; in gentler country
there were the villages with their ancient churches,
and often enough there were also more castles and
abbeys. Castles and churches ; there is hardly a
prospect in eighteenth-century literature that lacks
them, and in the few really remote parts without either,
Nature herself cannot please : the Peak, says Gray,
' is a country beyond comparison uglier than any other
I have seen in England, black, tedious, barren, and not
mountainous enough to please one with its horrors '.
The deeper truth, one may guess, is simply that it is
boring country because it lacks the evidences of history.
In less remote country, if the ancient castle were lacking,
it must be built. In the same letter (to Wharton, 4th
December 1762) Gray comments on a ' castle built only
for a plaything on the top of the hill '. Gray's severer
taste, and true knowledge of history, led him to scorn
such devices, but they were common enough. Horace
Walpole's Strawberry Hill is perhaps the most famous
example of the pseudo-antique, built in this case actually
to live in ; but the usual thing was to construct a ' ruin '.
Rousham Park in Oxfordshire, for example, the work
of Kent, lies on one side of a low valley, and on the
gentle slope opposite, a mile or two away, a ' ruin '
was built to complete the view. The whole effect is
reminiscent of a painting by Claude. The final touch
that was sometimes supplied by a rich man was the in-
stallation of a ' medieval ' hermit. There are instances
on record of men being payed to live in unwashed
solitude in cave or ruin, to provide the final effect of

medievalism for a rich man's guests. It was difficult, however, to keep them in employment for long.

Gray turns out to be less of an innovator than a perfect example. At the end of the seventeenth century Anne, Countess of Winchilsea, in her poem *Nocturnal Reverie* has an ' ancient Fabrick ' ; Collins in his *Ode to Evening* (1747) has a ' time hallow'd pile '. In 1744, Joseph Warton in his poem *The Enthusiast : or the Lover of Nature* lists among the delights of wild Nature ' spires and smoke emerging from the bosom of the grove ', and notes how the ' ruin'd tops of Gothick battlements appear '. Fielding had no fanciful eye for scenery, but when at the beginning of *Tom Jones* (1749) he describes the view from Mr. Allworthy's house (itself in noble ' Gothick ' style), he inevitably includes ' the towers of an old ruined Abbey, grown over with ivy, and part of the front '. William Mason in *The English Garden* (1) (1772) associates Nature with Time, describing scenes ' where Nature and where Time Have work'd congenial '. And he, too, naturally has ' Some mould'ring abbey's ivy-vested wall '.

It is tedious to multiply examples : a passage or two from Gilpin will clinch the matter and make a bridge to Wordsworth. The Reverend William Gilpin was the first professional tourist. He travelled with great enthusiasm over the British Isles, looking for picturesque scenery and describing it in guide-books intended to help other tourists and to form their taste for good composition in Nature. He encouraged the tourist to sketch admired views in water-colour, and wrote a poem of instruction entitled *Landscape Painting*. (The

connexion between literature and painting in the taste
for Nature and History is very close.) Whenever Gilpin
describes a typical and pleasing scene it goes like this:

> the winding river—the shooting promontory—the castle
> —the abbey—the flat distance—and the mountain melting
> into the horizon. (*Three Essays*, 1792, p. 85)

Even a totally barren landscape, says Gilpin, will supply
amusement—the various texture of the ground, the
changing light, cattle, birds: ' Even a winding road is
a thing of beauty '. But, he continues,

> if we let the imagination loose . . . the imagination can
> plant hills; can form rivers and lakes in vallies; can build
> castles and abbeys; and if it find no other amusement,
> can dilate itself in vast ideas of space.
>
> (*Three Essays*, pp. 55–6)

Wordsworth certainly knew some of Gilpin's works,
and this passage is probably echoed by one in *The
Prelude*. Put together they illustrate one another, and
show how different is Wordsworth's feeling for Nature
from ours. In *The Prelude* Wordsworth asks ' who
does not love to follow with his eye the windings of a
public way ', and he goes on to make a little clearer what
Gilpin says about space:

> the sight [of a winding public way],
> Familiar object as it is, hath wrought
> On my imagination since the morn
> Of childhood, when a disappearing line,
> One daily present to my eyes, that crossed
> The naked summit of a far-off hill
> Beyond the limits that my feet had trod,

> Was like an invitation into space
> Boundless, or guide into eternity.
>
> (Book XIII, ll. 143-51)

Would anyone nowadays find that the sight of a winding road led into ideas of eternity? The connexion made by Wordsworth is easy enough to follow, once made; but though most people would nowadays say that a winding road disappearing over a hill draws the mind attractively on, it is unlikely that the response would be the same as Gilpin's and Wordsworth's. Their response is genuine and natural, but it is likely that Wordsworth's was influenced by Gilpin, or by the set of ideas, climate of feeling, represented and fostered by Gilpin; and in any event, the response is one that is not typical either much before or much after the latter half of the eighteenth century.

Wordsworth's feeling for Nature is very much that of the second half of the eighteenth century. To call him a Romantic and to think (as he sometimes seems to have thought himself) that his feeling for Nature was something new is to misunderstand both the historical situation, and the essential quality of Wordsworth's poetry. The poetry is less *necessarily* concerned with Nature than is sometimes thought, as I shall show in the next section. Meanwhile, the association of History with Nature is as strong in Wordsworth as in his immediate predecessors. The causes are the same; the ruins scattered about England, and, increasingly in this last quarter of the eighteenth century, the weight of literary tradition. From the moment he was able to run about, the child Wordsworth was able to play in the ' green courts ' of the ruined castle at Cockermouth, one of his favourite haunts, set on the edge of the town, by green fields. At Cockermouth and Brougham Castle, says Mrs Moorman in her admirable biography, and in the ruins of Furness Abbey ' he had felt all the spell of antiquity in its ' Gothic ' manifestations ' (*Wordsworth: The Early Years*, 1957, p. 102). Much of his favourite reading emphasised the connexion between History and Nature. Beattie's *Minstrel* (1770 and 1774) early became one of his favourite poems, and remained a favourite all his life. It is a characteristic eighteenth century poem, rejoicing equally in natural scenery and in the apparatus of ' Gothic ' history, graves, ghosts, and ruins.

It is no wonder then that in one of the earliest of Wordsworth's poems, *The Vale of Esthwaite*, we find the mixture as before. He describes himself walking through the storm, catching glimpses of white torrents through the gloom, and being brought by them to think of how

> in his hall in times of yore
> Alone a Baron

sees ghosts at midnight hour. It is an extraordinary comparison to the modern reader, far-fetched and not worth the carrying, but perfectly ' natural ', granted the poet's youth, to his own time. Scott shows a similar type of feeling. How similar and how different from the Anglo-Saxon thrill of detestation at the gloomy storm, when the heavens weep !

The feeling for History is present in the very title of

that great poem about Nature *Lines written above Tintern Abbey* (1798).   Nature, in the eighteenth century, was truly itself when introduced under the shade of a ruined Abbey.   There is here another link with Gilpin. Wordsworth had with him on the energetic walking-tour in 1798 when he composed the poem a copy of Gilpin's *Tour of the Wye*, to which, as Mrs. Moorman points out (p. 402), the opening descriptive passage of the poem is slightly indebted.   Gilpin mentions the smoke rising above the trees from the charcoal furnaces : but this industrial note must have seemed too prosaic, and Wordsworth ' Gothicizes ' the smoke, and says it rises

> With some uncertain notice, as might seem
> Of vagrant dwellers in the houseless woods,
> Or of some Hermit's cave, where by his fire
> The Hermit sits alone.

The only hermit one could have met in the eighteenth century would have been one of those rarities already mentioned, employed by some rich man, as false and stagey as the ruins that were built to complete a view. The whole opening section of the *Lines written above Tintern Abbey*, with its painstaking and not very happy description, is as dull as any eighteenth-century ' land-scape ' poem.   Indeed, it is an eighteenth-century landscape poem.   It is better than most.   Apart from the trivial false note of the hermit it is honest, competent, and free from pompous diction ; but like so many of its *genre*, it is not very interesting.   The poem's greatness begins—and it is typical of Wordsworth's greatness in this—when the poet leaves the description of Nature and turns to the description of his own feeling.

There would be no point in tracing the interest in History in all of Wordsworth's poetry. The interest is constant and pervading, and is there to see for anyone who will read the poems, or even the titles. *The Prelude*, Wordsworth's greatest poem, is worth more consideration. It has an uncertain start, and only settles down to firm progress when Wordsworth turns to the description of the natural surroundings of his childhood, which was probably the first to be written down. The very first picture of these natural surroundings contains the inevitable reference to

> the shadow of those towers
> That yet survive, a shattered monument
> Of feudal sway.   (Book I, ll. 283–5)

When he tells how, as a schoolboy at Hawkshead, he raced with his friends in boats, one of the islands they sought had a ruined chapel dedicated to the Blessed Virgin. When they went further on expeditions on horseback it was to some Druid temple or the 'holy scene' of a ruined abbey.

It is time to ask what is the consequence of this association between Nature and History. And why is it so rarely noticed? Wordsworth's poetry in this as in other respects may be regarded as a climax to eighteenth-century developments of thought and feeling, and yet no one could claim that for all his frequency of historical reference Wordsworth powerfully represents the historical side of the two-fold concept of Nature-History. Each side was equally strong in

Gray; and in Wordsworth and Scott, who are his greatest successors in this way of feeling, the double concept persists. But the later writers responded more to one part than to the other. In Scott, the feeling for Nature, though genuine at bottom, is often falsified in his portrayal of the picturesque, and natural scenery is always quite external and objective to him. He excels in the feeling for History, (though only of comparatively recent history. His medievalism is as stagey as a constructed ruin). Wordsworth is the opposite to Scott. He feels strongly about Nature, and his feeling for History, though genuine, is a conventional response at a more superficial level of the mind.

Nevertheless the feeling for History is partly accountable, in all probability, for certain characteristics in Wordsworth's feeling for Nature. If one thinks of Nature simply as natural scenery, how extraordinary it seems that Nature should come to be regarded as a teacher : and how extraordinary that for Wordsworth ' love of Nature should lead to love of Man '! Taken at its face value, was there ever a sillier remark made than that

> One impulse from a vernal wood
> Will teach you more of man,
> Of moral evil and of good,
> Than all the sages can ?   (*The Tables Turned*)

Yet the feeling for History can partly account for this association between Nature and Man. The association between Nature and Man is obviously inherent in the association between Nature and History. History was not the only link, of course. Wordsworth's early sight of shepherds and knowledge of country people was clearly another formative influence. But it seems unlikely that this other influence would have been strong enough without the semi-philosophical implications and powerful sentiment which History helped to yoke to the feeling for Nature. The shepherds, the boyhood games, the decent life of lowly cottages, all combined with the ubiquitous and powerful force of History, to bring about a still further stage in ' humanising Nature '. For that is what the process amounts to in the eighteenth century, and it culminates in the poetry of Wordsworth. I have referred to the process of what has been called the ' divinization of Nature ', and Wordsworth himself talks at times of Nature in terms of religious veneration. But as far as literature and the feeling for natural scenery goes, the process can be more truly described as ' humanization ' than ' divinization '. At least Nature became a divinity which man, and especially Wordsworth, made in his own image. Terrible as Nature might seem to be at times to Wordsworth, it was with the terror of a severe nurse, of a high-minded schoolteacher, embodiments of his own conscience. Much as we may tremble in childhood (more then than now) before the ferocity of nurse, parent, or teacher, we rarely feel in it any alien, nonhuman quality. Disagreeable, bullying, reasonably or unreasonably stern as such guardians may be, they are yet human. So it is with Nature in Wordsworth's poetry. For a truly alien concept of Nature we must wait for nineteenth-century developments leading to Hardy and the middle novels of D. H. Lawrence. For Words-

worth Nature has been humanized by her association
with History and can thus become, like History, a
teacher of morals : associated with History, Nature is
naturally associated with ' the still, sad music of humanity '. For Wordsworth, Nature has taken over most of
the functions of History.

III

Wordsworth

But the process did not rest there. History had
helped to make a humanized Nature possible for Wordsworth.   In his conscious thought Wordsworth remained
at this point, reached at the end of the eighteenth
century, all his life.   It makes for a quite agreeable
presentation of natural scenery, though one whose
fascinations are paling rapidly.   How much more vital
is Lawrence's response to external nature.   But as
Wordsworth says, love of Nature led him to love of
Man ; and love of Man for Wordsworth is knowledge
of himself.   There are two levels in Wordsworth's
poetry (rather corresponding to the famous ' two
voices ') : one is the superficial level of Nature poetry ;
the other a deeper level when outward things fall from
him, and he is moving about, fearful and guilty and
wondering, among the unrealised depths of his own
mind.   It is on this deeper level that Wordsworth is
a great poet.   His eighteenth-century view of Nature
led him down to it, Nature was, by the accidents of
his life and time, the intermediary to it, but Nature had
essentially no place in it.   If it had, we who do not live

in the Lake District at the end of the eighteenth century would find it as hard to appreciate Wordsworth's great poetry, as we do to appreciate the vastly greater quantity of minor poetry that he continued to pour out all his life.

It is no accident that Wordsworth is the first writer recorded as using the word *self-respect* in its modern sense. Before him the word meant ' a *wrongful* regard for oneself '. Keats's phrase ' the egotistical sublime ' has always been rightly regarded as a true key to Wordsworth's essential power. At his greatest he is an obsessional writer, and as usual in such cases, the obsession is not merely with himself, a mere vanity, but with his experiences as a child.

The quality of his obsession is to some extent obscured from us, as no doubt it was to him, by the very love of Nature as a local mode of sensibility, a convention, which he acquired from the literary tradition and his own country boyhood. Furthermore, Wordsworth knew, or thought he knew, that his boyhood had been a happy one, because of his communion with Nature. His most recent biographer emphasises the happiness, and we need not quarrel with her judgment. But happiness is no more simple than other feelings. We tend to think that there are a rather small number of identifiable feelings, love, hate, fear, misery, happiness, and so forth. But these are only very general classes of feeling; each one can take on a thousand different shapes and colours and combinations. One of the chief functions of literature is by a process of ' incarnation ' in story and image, to locate and describe, to explore and make more generally available, some of these possible feelings. (Literary criticism, in its more modest and derivative way, has a similar chief function : it follows after the work of literature as literature follows after experience ; literature works on experience and criticism works on literature (not forgetting experience). If the poets, novelists, dramatists, are the fighting troops, the critics are the second-line troops who come up after the hill-top is won, and trace its outline in detail, consolidate the position, defend it against the counterattacks of time, ignorance, blank inattention, preconceived ideas, and dulled sensibilities.)

To understand Wordsworth's poetry at its best we must understand the nature of his obsession with his own childhood : and to understand that, we do best to examine *The Prelude* where he avowedly treats his own childhood most directly. And though he talks so much about Nature we do best for a while to disregard what he says about Nature, especially as it is always difficult, significantly enough, to know quite what he means by Nature.

Wordsworth began *The Prelude* at Goslar in Germany in the winter of 1798–9, and completed practically the whole of the first book except the first 270 lines. Besides a few small lyrics he also composed the fragment *Nutting*, published in the second edition of *The Lyrical Ballads* and equally reminiscent of boyhood.

What is notable about this first book of *The Prelude* (less the first 270 lines), and about *Nutting* is the predominant force of the images of guilt and desertion. There are of course passages about joy in Nature, ' vulgar joy ', as Wordsworth calls it (l. 581), and joy in the society of the lowly cottages in which as a schoolboy he was boarded out with his brothers and friends. These passages are important, but they have if anything received too much stress from Wordsworth himself and his critics : or rather, perhaps, the images of guilt and desertion have not received, in comparison with these others, their fair due. The three passages which were the very first to be composed are *Nutting*, the episode of the stolen boat, and the account of skating by starlight. Only this last is free from guilt. In the first book of *The Prelude* the first image of his childhood that is recorded is the brief description of his birthplace, with the conventional connexion of Nature and History already noted (above, p. 171). This has no stamp of personal childhood memory. Immediately following comes the account of his visiting his snares by night as a boy. This is a typical image of guilt. The stars shone, and

> I was alone,
> And seemed to be a trouble to the peace
> That dwelt among them. (*Prelude* (1850), I. 315–17)

Sometimes he stole someone else's capture,

> and when the deed was done
> I heard among the solitary hills
> Low breathings coming after me, and sounds
> Of undistinguishable motion, steps
> Almost as silent as the turf they trod. (ll. 321–5)

This is surely an interesting first communion with Nature! For though it is obviously not his first conscious recollection of natural scenery it has primary place in what Mr. Eliot has called ' the logic of the imagination ' that governs the poem. Next follows an account of birds-nesting—an object, says Wordsworth, ' mean and inglorious ' though no sense of guilt is expressed. Instead, he tells of the delicious sense of danger ' while on the perilous ridge I hung alone '. How strange, he continues, three or four lines later

> that all
> The terrors, pains, and early miseries,
> Regrets, vexations, lassitudes interfused
> Within my mind, should e'er have borne a part,
> And that a needful part, in making up
> The calm existence that is mine when I
> Am worthy of myself!   (ll. 344–50)

No doubt some of the early miseries are attributable to the disagreeable grandparents at Penrith who looked after the Wordsworth children when their mother died. But the placing of this passage close to the others suggests that the source of unhappiness was deeper. And one might argue that when Wordsworth wrote this passage his own deepest need at the time was to dredge up these longburied terrors and pains, and the obscure feelings of guilt and desertion which accompanied them, from the bottom of his mind, to bring them up to the light of day and so to set them at rest.

The Prelude then proceeds to tell the famous story of how he stole the boat at night and was pursued by the grim shape of the avenging mountain:

> after I had seen
> That spectacle, for many days, my brain
> Worked with a dim and undetermined sense

Of unknown modes of being; o'er my thoughts
There hung a darkness, call it solitude
Or *blank desertion*.   No familiar shapes
Remained, no pleasant images of trees,
Of sea or sky, no colours of green fields;
But huge and mighty forms, that do not live
Like living men, moved slowly through the mind
By day, and were a trouble to my dreams.

      (ll. 390–400. *Itali s mine.*)

This magnificent passage is deeply characteristic of
Wordsworth in more ways than one.   But at the moment
I want to emphasise the sense of guilt.   It is obviously
grossly disproportionate to the petty crime, as is the
sense of guilt which makes him feel, before he has even
stolen anything, that he is a trouble to the peace of the
stars.   Sensitive child as he no doubt was, there is clearly
something deeper in his mind, of which these peccadil-
loes are mere representatives.   And thus, as will be
found whenever Wordsworth is most deeply moved,
Nature becomes for him, not an external pleasurable
or stimulating environment, but the very pattern of
his mind.   The huge and mighty forms take their shape
from the mountains, but their life they take from
Wordsworth's own mind.   There is also in this passage
the strange reference to the sense of desertion.   It is
apparently caused by the sense of loss of ' familiar
shapes ', but it is a strange emotion to be associated
with crime, however great or petty.

The other passage, written about this time, *Nutting*,
again repeats the feeling of guilt though on a more superficial level :

> I felt a sense of pain when I beheld
> The silent trees and saw the intruding sky.

Here he rationalises the guilt, as is perhaps suggested by the hesitant lines

> unless I now
> Confound my present feelings with the past.

He is either not sure whether he did feel at the time the pain at spoiling the trees, or is not sure if he has the true reason for his sense of guilt.

This sense of guilt and sometimes desertion is not the only sensation he connects with his intercourse with nature, but it is certainly his earliest. The earliest recollection in *The Prelude*, says Mrs. Moorman, is probably that other great passage when he tells how he was stricken with ' the visionary dreariness ' of Penrith Beacon, when according to Wordsworth he was five years old. It is typical of the structure of *The Prelude* that this passage occurs in Book XII and is linked with another episode that occurred when he was thirteen years old.

It will be remembered how, when he could scarcely ride, he went out on a horse with a servant. He somehow became separated from the man, and being too nervous to continue riding, dismounted. He came to a spot where a murder had been committed and the murderer had been later hung ; recognising the place by some initials carved on the turf, he fled terrified,

> Faltering and faint, and ignorant of the road :
> Then, reascending the bare common, saw
> A naked pool that lay beneath the hills,

The beacon on the summit, and, more near,
A girl, who bore a pitcher on her head,
And seemed with difficult step to force her way
Against the blowing wind. It was, in truth,
An ordinary sight: but I should need
Colours and words that are unknown to man,
To paint the visionary dreariness
Which, while I looked all round for my lost guide,
Invested moorland waste, and naked pool . . .

(ll. 247-58)

The scene is not the ' nature ' of an ordinary nature
lover. And when Wordsworth describes scenes like
this, obviously deeply felt personal memories, he
emancipates himself from the eighteenth-century tradition of nature-poetry—and shows himself, too, unconnected with the nature-poetry of the nineteenth and
twentieth centuries, the close observations of elm-
flowers of a Tennyson, the village-green cricket and
pastoral sweetness of the Georgians. There is nothing
very obviously attractive in the scene Wordsworth
paints here, and as usual with his best work, all is drawn
in broad sweeps. And again as usual what is notable
is the way the scene is infused with his own feelings.
The most obvious feeling here is desertion—the lost
guide—and the consequent desolation on a bare hillside.
The other obvious feeling is fear, the boyish fear of a
sinister place, where a crime was committed and two
lives cut short. It is not fanciful to detect in this last
a kind of imaginative participation in the murderer's
guilt. Childhood, uncertain of its own personality,
can as easily associate itself with the criminal as with the

hero; and always to some extent associates itself with strongly imagined personalities. My own children are both frightened by the wolves and ogres of fairy-stories, and ready to impersonate them in play.

The element of guilt, equally illogical and equally comprehensible, appears in the other episode of later life which is linked to the experience on Penrith Beacon. After a comment to which I shall return Wordsworth goes on to tell how when he was thirteen, he eagerly and impatiently waited at the beginning of the school holidays for the horses that would take him and his brother home. The scene is characteristically Wordsworthian—a bleak hill-side; a dry-stone wall through which the wind whistled; nearby a single sheep, one blasted hawthorn; images of solitude and endurance like the girl on Penrith Beacon, the leechgatherer, and many another in Wordsworth's work. This time the emotions that fill the scene are drawn from the immediate future which succeeded it, and which saw the death of his father. And characteristically, the death of his father seemed a ' chastisement ' to the boy. That was, as the adult Wordsworth knew, a trite moralization, but nevertheless he could not but feel there had been something wrong in his eager expectation: to the scene is attached a sense of guilt. And perhaps we may add, too, desertion: for his father had died, and the death of loved ones may easily be felt by children as a desertion.

Indeed, if there were any point here in mere biographical speculation we might well wonder if this pervasive sense of guilt and desertion in Wordsworth

were not intimately connected with his mother's death
when he was eight years old. She was clearly an impressive woman; he loved her dearly, and he remembered very clearly at least one rebuke. He says
of her death, ' She left us destitute ' (*Prelude*, V, l. 259).
In the love-hate complex which constitutes every child's
relation to his parents, it is also not impossible for a child
to feel that the death of a parent is due to his own rebellion and illwill. But images of desertion may derive
from our expulsion from the womb or from numberless
frequent and trivial passages of child life. Deserted, even
betrayed, we must all be, in the very process of growing
up. There is no point in attempting to examine so
closely Wordsworth's own life. What is important is
that he could express his sense of desertion, and that
we can respond it: that in expressing it Wordsworth
eased himself of a burden, and that in following Wordsworth's expression we too may be eased of our burdens.

An interesting episode in which Wordsworth's almost
neurotic anxiety and sense of desertion strongly appears is the famous dream (Book V, ll. 56–140) about
the Arab who was also Don Quixote, who was trying to
save the science and the poetry of the world from a
new Flood. Here again, the Arab-Quixote deserts
Wordsworth in the waste of the world, and Wordsworth
wakes in terror as the ' fleet waters of the drowning
world ' follow in chase. Mrs Moorman considers that
the anxiety and fear of this dream place it unmistakably
after his French experiences (*Early Life*, p. 250). But
as I have shown, anxiety and fear were clearly rooted
in his childhood. It is a childhood experience to listen

to the ' sea ' in a shell. Wordsworth could have read
Cervantes among his father's books, and early at school
came upon Euclid. It may well have been a dream of
quite early adolescence. At whatever age it occurred,
the emotional pattern of anxiety and desertion is typical
of Wordsworth.

I have emphasised the sensations of guilt and desertion
in Wordsworth's childhood because they are usually
neglected, because they set something of a pattern in
Wordsworth's life, and because his dwelling on them
leads to the secret of his power. The pattern they set
comes out most clearly in the major crisis of his life,
centred on his experiences in France. The final result
of his stay in France was a period of such painful disil-
lusion and sorrow that it may be regarded as almost a
nervous breakdown. The state lasted in greater or
less intensity, and with numerous intermissions, from
1793 to well on into the Racedown period (1795–7),
though by the spring of 1797 he seems to have recovered.

His distress had several causes, both personal and
general. His early joy in the French Revolution had
been marred by the British declaration of war on France,
which was a bitter blow to him. The French Revolution itself turned to the horror of the murderous ex-
cesses of the Jacobins. And further associated with
France was his love-affair with Annette Vallon, by
whom he had a daughter, and whom the political situation and his own lack of money and prospects prevented
from marrying.

This last more personal distress has been much over-
emphasised. There can be no doubt that it contributed

to Wordsworth's complicated feelings of misery, guilt
and betrayal. He had had every intention of marrying
Annette. It was no vulgar seduction. But we must
not bring the moral attitudes of the later nineteenth
century novel to bear upon this unfortunate and indeed
shameful episode. It was no surprising thing for a
young man of the middle classes to have a lovechild.
At one time William and Dorothy Wordsworth while
at Racedown proposed looking after a natural daughter
of their cousin, Tom Myers. At much the same period,
and in circles no less respectable, it is thought in *Sense
and Sensibility* that Colonel Brandon himself, a virtuous
enough character, has a love-child. The Dashwoods,
and Jane Austen herself, spinster and virtuous woman,
are neither shocked nor surprised. And just as there
was no especial opprobrium directed to the father, there
seems to have been none of the late-nineteenth and early-
twentieth century's wicked discrimination against an
illegitimate child. Wordsworth's friend Basil Montagu
was illegitimate, though admittedly his father was a lord.
(In aristocratic or even upper-middle class society there
was of course even less restraint. When Shelley went
to Oxford, his father told him he would not mind a
love-affair, but would not stand for an unconven-
tional marriage.) In these matters, as in all others,
different ages of the same racial culture take different
views. It would be possible to trace the condemnation
of bastardy rising and falling in English literature from
an early period. The Elizabethan and Jacobean period
saw a high point in condemnation (in Shakespeare a
bastard is *bound* to be a villain); and so did the latter

part of the nineteenth century and the early part of the twentieth.   But in the early nineteenth century the heavy pall of Victorian ' respectability ' had not fallen.

We need not therefore suppose that Wordsworth was excessively distressed only by his separation from Annette and the fact that she had had a child by him. Nor, as Mrs. Moorman shows, did he ever refuse to acknowledge his relationship with both, either to Dorothy or his wife.   The evidence of his passionate interest in politics throughout his life, and what he himself says in *The Prelude* about France, for Wordsworth was not a liar, are sufficient to show that the course of political events, especially when *combined* with his affair with Annette, was well able to produce the misery he describes himself as suffering.

In Wordsworth's imaginative life this period of distress and his recovery from it is the major theme.   All the rationalisation about Nature, about the Imagination, about Man, all centre on this major series of events, that he grew, he was blighted, he recovered.   This is the account he himself gives of the course of his life, under the image of a stream :

> we have traced the stream
> From the blind cavern whence is faintly heard
> Its natal murmur ; followed it to light
> And open day ; accompanied its course
> Among the ways of Nature, for a time
> Lost sight of it bewildered and engulphed ;
> Then given it greeting as it rose once more
> In strength, reflecting from its placid breast
> The works of man and face of human life . . .
>
>   (Book XIV, ll. 194–202)

The period of crisis is just that period, as Mrs. Moorman shows (*Early Life*, p. 237) which he describes in *Lines written above Tintern Abbey*, where he sought nature

> *more like a man*
> *Flying from something that he dreads*, than one
> Who sought the thing he loved.

In this last is again the curious touch of fear and guilt which is in Wordsworth's deepest response to nature. The crisis itself is described in the tenth book of *The Prelude*. Wordsworth describes his misery at the state of affairs in France herself, at having to leave France, and at the shame of England's declaration of war on France. He tells how the memory of the atrocities of the French Revolution haunted him for years after, and he dreamt continually of the innocent victims in their dungeons:

> Then suddenly the scene
> Changed, and the unbroken dream entangled me
> In long orations, which I strove to plead
> Before unjust tribunals,—with a voice
> Labouring, a brain confounded, *and a sense*,
> *Death-like, of treacherous desertion*, felt
> In the last place of refuge—my own soul.
> (Book X, ll. 409–15)

In the 1805 version of *The Prelude* the last two lines read

> *Of treachery and desertion* in the place
> The holiest that I knew of, my own soul. (ll. 380–1)

This passage is as it were the pivot of *The Prelude*. The crisis was protracted in his own life, and though ' telescoped ' as regards time in *The Prelude* is portrayed somewhat indistinctly, being overlayed with a good deal of moralization and meditation after the event. The crisis brought about by the loss of his hopes for France, England, and Annette, repeated the form of earlier experiences. In this French crisis, as in the earlier experiences, Wordsworth was dominated by the sense of guilt and desertion. The association between the two elements suggests that the desertion itself was dual. He felt deserted by his own ideals, his own hopes; but that he felt guilty also implies that he felt that he himself had deserted—something, or someone. What or whom had he deserted or betrayed? Not Annette alone, and not Annette first of all. It would be possible to argue that Wordsworth imposed a sense of his own guilt and failure aquired in this major crisis of early manhood on to the experiences of childhood. But Wordsworth's own honesty, and a general knowledge of human nature would suggest the opposite: that the pattern of crisis experienced in earliest childhood imposed itself on, or found a natural opportunity in, the more conscious crisis of manhood. The earlier experiences were both models and rehearsals for the later one.

There is nothing unusual in such a situation. Our earlier experiences always determine to some extent what later experiences are possible to us, and Wordsworth seems to have had an obscure intuition of this. And because of this it is often possible to perceive a rough pattern in a man's life, and especially in an artist's life, since he is always attempting to realise his inner pattern on the outside world, on

> all the mighty world
> Of eye, and ear,—both what they half create,
> And what perceive.

It is, too, usually easier to perceive such a pattern in the work of ' obsessive ' artists. In Milton the obsession with temptation—temptation, moreover, successfully resisted—is to be seen in *Lycidas, Comus, Paradise Regained, Samson Agonistes*. It is to be found in *Paradise Lost* in Satan's successful, rather Graham Greene-ish temptation to be virtuous. (The only case in Milton's work where temptation is not successfully resisted is that of Adam and Eve, and at that point of his great poem his art is correspondingly less successful.) In D. H. Lawrence the polarity between his vital un-intellectual father, coming up from the dark pit, black with coal-dust, on the one side ; and on the other side his agressive, intellectual, dominating mother, living clean and above the ground, works through all his writings from *Sons and Lovers* onwards. So in Words-worth the obsessive pattern of his childhood works through all his major poetry. The rest of his poetry is more willed : it is the fruit of his desire to be a poet, and is correspondingly less successful, though it is not all negligible.

What is important, of course, is that Wordsworth recovered from his major crisis. *The Prelude*, as he is continually saying, is a poem of ' renovation '. In the first 54 lines of *The Prelude*, he concludes by describing himself as 'A renovated spirit ' (l. 53).

The source of power that Wordsworth rediscovered to build his shattered life was not, basically, the influence of either Dorothy or Nature. I do not underrate the importance of their influence, but they were essentially intermediaries. The true source of his recovery Wordsworth himself knew, if only by glimpses. His clearest statement comes characteristically interposed between the memories of the scene of ' visionary dreariness ' at Penrith Beacon and the equally dreary scene of his anxious wait to return home just before his father died. He breaks out

> Oh ! mystery of man, from what a depth
> Proceed thy honours. I am lost but see
> In simple childhood something of the base
> On which thy greatness stands : but this I feel,
> That *from thyself it comes*, that thou must give,
> Else never canst receive. The days gone by
> Return upon me almost from the dawn
> Of life : the hiding places of man's power
> Open ; I would approach them, but they close.
> I see by glimpses now ; when age comes on,
> May scarcely see at all ; . . .
>
> (Book XII, ll. 272–82)

No lover of Wordsworth (love is a curious word to use for such an unattractive personality, but how else can we express our sense of veneration and gratitude for his power ?) needs to be told of Wordsworth's obsession with childhood. But we have known Wordsworth so long as a ' nature-poet ' that we underestimate the full importance of his continual return to the theme, even though Coleridge saw it so clearly.

Wordsworth finds the source of man's power in his capacity to release the vital energies stored in the

memories of childhood. *The Prelude* is an exercise in
depth psychology, a kind of self-therapy, leading to re-
integration of the personality. Wordsworth elsewhere
emphasises that the source of power lies in man himself,
not Nature; significantly one of these passages comes a
little after he has described the nadir of his misery in
the dreams in which he himself was accused, in the
passage already quoted:

> Then was the truth received into my heart
> That, under heaviest sorrow earth can bring,
> (Griefs bitterest of ourselves or of our kind,)
> If from the affliction somewhere do not grow
> Honour which could not else have been, a faith,
> An elevation, and a sanctity,
> If new strength be not given, nor old restored,
> The blame is our's, not Nature's.
>
> (Book X, ll. 464–70)

The line in parenthesis, with its revealing personal note,
comes from the 1805 version, and was cut out of the
1850 version.

The importance of Nature and of Dorothy to Wordsworth lies very largely in their being intermediaries to
the memory of his childhood. The intense experiences
of his childhood found their form in the memories of
the outer world upon which he, like all of us, imposed
the patterns of his feelings. Natural scenery, in other
words, was for Wordsworth, in actual experience as
well as in art, an ' objective correlative '. His dwelling
upon the natural scenes of his childhood enabled him
to recreate the deeper sensations which had been, and
necessarily must continue to be, the source of his deepest

imaginative vitality, of his real inner life, above and beyond the mere continuation of his bodily functions.

Why should these deeper sensations have such renovative power? Perhaps because so many of them were composed at least partly of feelings of guilt and betrayal, and that to recognise them as such was to release energy which might otherwise have been wasted in repressing them. If so, it would be a familiar process. But even if this is true, there were also other reasons. Wordsworth himself suggests one after the account of the childish experience on Penrith Beacon.

> So feeling comes in aid
> Of feeling, and diversity of strength
> Attends us, *if but once we have been strong.*
>
> (Book XII, ll. 269–71)

He had *endured* the early terrors, the ' severer interventions '; he had even in a sense withstood them. And when the later crisis came upon him, he could hope, by past experience, to recover by simple endurance. How many images haunt his poetry of pathetic, feeble, destitute persons, who in their very weakness exemplify the astonishing capacity of men to endure, and in whom mere endurance itself is a triumph : the old soldier in Book IV of *The Prelude*; the blind beggar in Book VII ; the Leechgatherer ; the Cumberland Beggar ; Simon Lee ; even the Highland Reaper. And lastly, the images of early life were associated, too, with other images which up to now I have made little mention of, because they are so well known, the ' gentler visitations ' of Nature. For as everyone knows, Wordsworth's childhood, underlain as it was by anxiety and fear mediated through the forms of nature, also contained much that was normal, cheerful and delightful. Perhaps the more attractive scenes of Nature never made such a profound appeal to Wordsworth as did the wild, desolate or the stormy. But obvious beauty and the ministrations of Dorothy could and did play their part in soothing and helping him.

In this connexion it was Dorothy's sharper eye for detail and clearer memory for the smaller sights and sounds of nature that also helped Wordsworth. She is the clear counterpart of his more superficial, conventional, day-to-day intercourse with nature, as well as being a bond with his childhood. In his address to her at the end of *The Prelude* Wordsworth says

> For, spite of thy sweet influence and the touch
> Of kindred hands that opened out the springs
> Of genial thought in childhood, . . .
> *I too exclusively esteemed that love*
> *And sought that beauty, which, as Milton sings,*
> *Hath terror in it. Thou didst soften down*
> *This over-sternness* . . .

(Book XIV, ll. 237–47)

His soul he says was like a rock with torrents roaring; Dorothy planted its crevices with flowers and so forth.

It is important now to distinguish more clearly these two levels of response to Nature in Wordsworth's poetry. This will involve a simplification, but not falsification. The passage just quoted, along with others quoted in this essay, suggest that Wordsworth's deeper response was to Nature which, if beautiful, is also terrible. His more superficial response is to Nature in her pleasanter moods. The deeper response is also

to the more general aspects of Nature—the grand sweep
of the hills, the large turmoil of the storm, those aspects
in fact, which can be suffused with personal feeling.
The more superficial response is conveyed in the more
detailed notice of scenery, like the opening of *The Lines
written above Tintern*.   Interest in details was what was
characteristic of Dorothy, as any reader of her *Journal*
knows.   Such an interest was for Wordsworth an
aesthetic or scientific interest, ' extrinsic passion ', and
he distrusted it in himself at least, for all his tributes to
Dorothy.   It is characteristic that Wordsworth says of
himself, in condemnation, at the time of his deepest
crisis, when his sense of deeper communion with Nature
was lost, that he looked at Nature without any interest
' unborrowed from the eye '.   Such an interest was
exactly that of Gilpin and of many another eighteenth-
or nineteenth-century admirer of the beauty of Nature,
from Gray onwards.   It was Wordsworth's boyhood
interest, a ' collateral interest ', an ' extrinsic passion '.

Wordsworth's deeper feeling for Nature is something
very different.   For one thing, it is all but independent
of the senses, except for sight, and quite without detail.
It is a direct apprehension of ' dream-like vision and
splendour '—Mrs. Moorman has most usefully collected
a number of references (*Early Life*, p. 41).   The vision
characterises all the greater moments of his communion
with Nature, especially those moments associated with
guilt and anxiety.   The deeper response is described
again in the great *Ode on the Intimations of Immortality*
where the lack of sensuous detail is even emphasised,
and what are praised are

> those obstinate questionings
> Of sense and outward things,
> Fallings from us, vanishings;
> Blank misgivings of a Creature
> Moving about in worlds not realised,
> High instincts before which our mortal Nature
> *Did tremble like a guilty Thing* surprised.   (ll. 145–51)

Here, for once, Wordsworth has expressed himself untrammelled by nature imagery, and gets to the core of the matter; the strange intuitions of his childhood. In a famous passage of recollection when he was an old man he said of such states,

> I was often unable to think of external things as having external existence, *and I communed with all I saw as something not apart from but inherent in my own immaterial nature.*
>
> (Quoted in *Early Life*, p. 41. *Italics mine.*)

Here we have the core of the matter. Wordsworth's greatest writing about Nature, in *The Prelude*, in *Tintern Abbey*, in the *Intimations*, and less obviously in other poems, is that which only uses the larger outward forms of nature to embody the ' unknown modes of being ' deep within his own soul: where the hills and mists, the very heavenly bodies, become a representation of his own mind. This is not ' the pathetic fallacy '. He does not attribute his own conscious feelings to natural objects or creatures. But his own *otherwise unrecognisable* feelings are embodied in his mental vision like mountains, ' huge and mighty forms ' that moved slowly through the mind.

One of the greatest passages of *The Prelude* practically recognises this faculty in himself of so objectifying the ' shape ' of his mind in the form of mountain and cloud. It is the marvellous account of his climb up Snowdon at the beginning of Book XIV, when he suddenly broke through the low-lying clouds and mist and saw in clear moonlight the ' dusky backs ' of a hundred hills, and heard the thunder of the waters arising from below. When the vision had partially dissolved, he says,

> it appeared to me the type
> Of a majestic intellect, . . .

(Book XIV, ll. 66–7)

The majestic intellect was that of Wordsworth.

And here is the source of the powerful compulsion that *The Prelude* especially must maintain over all for whom poetry is a source of life: for whom poetry is more than the history of thought and feeling, or an adornment, or a pastime. *The Prelude* is a muddled poem: much in it is prosy: most of the superficial response to Nature is impossible in the twentieth century. But it goes deep into the mind of one man, and touches on unknown modes of being. And it shows the process of recovery from despair, guilt, desertion, which must inevitably accompany any process of growth. In following Wordsworth as he gropes down, however uncertainly, into these common depths of the mind, so we by sympathetic participation can follow out the process in our own minds, perhaps the more successfully that our needs may be almost unrecognised by ourselves. It was not a merely nineteenth century taste for ' nature-poetry ' that led J. S. Mill to recover from a nervous breakdown by reading Wordsworth's poetry, and led Arnold to write of Wordsworth's 'healing power '. It was a recognition of deepest needs. Has any other poet ever had such a therapeutic effect? It is because Wordsworth had healed himself.

This last reflection may suggest why Wordsworth after he had finished *The Prelude* and associated poems in the wonderful decade 1797–1807 never produced a further great body of work. He had finished his great subject. Guilt and sorrow, desertion, the solitude of the soul, endurance, these are his great themes and underlie his great poems; the most moving of his recurring images are those of the weak, the poor, the sorrowful, who nevertheless endure. Once he had exhausted these themes in *The Prelude* and other poems of much the same date, once he had traced them to the greatness and feebleness of childhood, what else had he to write about? Nature divorced from his great personal themes had no profound interest. The truth is that Wordsworth is not *essentially* a ' nature poet '. No great poet is.

E. M. FORSTER AND SAWSTON:
THE DIVIDED MIND

The basis of all Mr. Forster's novels is the upper
section of English suburban middle-class society, living
on the fringes of London, about 1900. The class of
society is that which sent its sons to minor public
schools, and which provided higher Civil Servants,
Colonial and Imperial administrators, stockbrokers in
the City of London, directors of steady, long-established
businesses, and university dons at Oxford and Cambridge. It is clearly the class of society from which
Mr. Forster himself springs. In his novels he never
strays out of it, as far as *English* society goes; though
he goes to the extreme edge of it with Stephen Wonham,
the uneducated farmer in *The Longest Journey*, and
Leonard Bast, the poor clerk, in *Howards End*; and
Stephen is very unconvincing, and Leonard Bast only
partly convincing.

It is important to localise this class of society in time
and place, because it is so central to all the novels, so
important to Mr. Forster's imagination, and because it
has in its original form ceased to exist. Many of its
young men were killed in 1914; between the wars it
was eroded by new ideas and attitudes such as socialism,
communism, by the vast implications of psychoanalysis,
and by the world's events of depressions and wars. The
Education Act of 1944; the further acts of the Labour

Government of 1945–50 which brought in the ' Welfare
State ' ; punitive taxation ; the impossibility of obtain-
ing servants ; all these, confusing the classes and
making real leisure impossible for almost everyone,
have pretty well destroyed, as a class, the social group
Mr. Forster was born into. This group lives, in *The
Longest Journey*, at a place called Sawston, and Sawston
I shall proceed to call it, summing up in the word all
the people, their modest wealth, their leisure, and their
attitudes.

Sawston was especially that part of the nation which
' ran ' the whole country, not as in a dictatorship, but
as being responsible for guiding, not ruling, the complex machinery of a modern state. England, as George
Orwell has noted, is characteristically a country that is
' run '. (Incidentally Orwell, although he went to
Eton, was also a product of Sawston and his books and
essays are illuminating in their similarity and contrast
to Mr. Forster's.) The capacity for management, for
getting things done, or at least for keeping things
moving, is a virtue which the English naturally respect.
And Mr. Forster pays it its due, especially in the commercial field in *Howards End*, and more doubtfully in
the imperial field, in *A Passage to India*. But he is
much more concerned with the deficiencies of Sawston
than its virtues. The deficiencies are many, but may
be summed up, as several critics have noted, under the
theme of ' the undeveloped heart ', the failure to love.
Mr. Forster is not thinking primarily of sexual love, of
course, for he is not much interested in love between
a young man and a young woman ; he is thinking of love

as a general attitude of hearty, honest affection towards mankind, a feeling without pity, without sentimentality, capable even of cruelty, and above all spontaneous and genuine. Were Mr. Forster not anti-Christian one might easily call it Christian love, (the medieval virtue of *caritas*, love of one's neighbour), in a somewhat secularized form. Mr. Forster attributes the general Sawstonian lack of this quality of love to the English public school, for ' the undeveloped heart ' is especially an English upper-middle-class quality, not shared by the lower-class—not at any rate, until a few years ago, when the social classes began to be mingled together.

Another notable characteristic of Sawston was that it travelled far more extensively than any other section of English society. (It is of course upon Sawston that foreigners' ideas about the English are mostly based —the pipes, the tweeds, the impassivity, the incapacity to understand a foreign language, the often unconscious arrogance, the modest wealth and comfort, the clannishness, the incorruptibility, the passion for cleanliness. It is now an old-fashioned idea of the typical Englishman.) The travelling of Sawston is essential to several of Mr. Forster's novels, including his first, *Where Angels Fear to Tread*, and his last and greatest, *A Passage to India*.

The essence of *Where Angels Fear to Tread* is the clash between Sawstonian ideals and the experience of Italy. The suburban families of Sawston are accustomed to visit Italy for the beauty of Italian art and of the Italian countryside. But Mr. Forster's accusation is that they do so only because of a sense of obligation to

' culture '. Their appreciation of the countryside is
tepid, and they often disapprove of the nudity of the
art and the crudity of the people. Such disapproving
visitors have characteristically ' undeveloped hearts '.
But to certain members of these families Italy shows,
and arouses in them, true warmth of feeling, and a new,
passionate life. Mr. Forster can and does easily criticise
the faults of the Italians, their venality, irresponsibility,
cruelty, bad taste. But the Italians are excusable because they have warm hearts, they are passionately alive,
they really love and really hate, with spontaneity,
freshness, sincerity ; without caution (which in personal
relationships Mr. Forster always despises), without
meanness and spite. So to certain chosen members of
Sawston Italy brings an awakening, painful in some
ways, but beneficial. Awakening may seem disillusion-
ment, but only because we have to abandon what is false.
He writes

> Romance only dies with life. No pair of pincers will
> ever pull it out of us. But there is a spurious sentiment
> which cannot resist the unexpected and incongruous and
> the grotesque. A touch will loosen it, and the sooner it
> goes from us the better. It was going from Philip now,·
> and therefore he gave a cry of pain.

The concern with *spurious sentiment*, the false, is always
important in Mr. Forster's work. So is the other
element associated in this novel with Italy—the effect
of Nature. Sawston is incapable of true feeling and is
entangled in false because it is cut off from the natural
life of the earth. The Italian landscape, beautifully
described, is an important part of the book. The

general theme of the novel, then, is the confrontation of
Sawston with true natural passion, and true passionate
nature. Two of the Sawstonian characters, Philip and
Caroline, respond as best they may. The response is
not much, but it wins our sympathy. Those who do
not respond win nothing but our dislike and contempt.
There is no pity in Mr. Forster for those who are wrong.

The next novel is *The Longest Journey*. This time
the scene is set entirely in England. Although the
general theme is the same as before, the confrontation
of Sawston is more complex. Sawston is confronted
by two different opposing forces. One force is Cambridge, representing the true life of the mind; and the
other is the old pastoral England, which so haunts the
minds of men who grew up in the late nineteenth century
like Mr. Forster and D. H. Lawrence, who saw it being
destroyed before their very eyes. In other words,
Sawston is confronted by Mind and Nature. Of course
none of these forces is simple. I would not give the
impression of Mr. Forster as a writer of *romans à thèse*.
It may even be that he is not himself fully aware of the
dominant pattern that runs through all his work, though
he is a highly self-conscious writer. The general
theme is in most cases fully worked out in terms of
particular character and event. Of the complex associations of Sawston I have already suggested something. The force of Mind, represented by Cambridge,
is also complex, if not equally so. It implies a group
of persons, all men, devoted to the disinterested search
for Reality, living in beautiful buildings a sane ordered
decent modest life of learning, conversation, moderate

exercise, unseduced by the false charms of ambition or the vanities of high society. The other force, Nature, is in these early books primarily the appearance of a beautiful countryside, whether in England or Italy. But Nature, as so often with the English, is closely connected with a strong historical feeling, age-old pieties, and in Mr. Forster's case, a very nineteenth-century concept of ancient religions. In Italy Nature is the abode of Pan, who also (in a short story) turns up in England, too. In *The Longest Journey* Nature means Wiltshire, a part of that Salisbury Plain where Wordsworth once had a vision of ancient Druid rites. Like Wordsworth, too, Mr. Forster's feeling for Nature is closely connected with his love and respect for the ancient yeoman stock of independent farmers.

The three elements in *The Longest Journey* are represented by the three chief characters. Sawston is represented by the hero Rickie; Cambridge by the philosophical Stewart Ansell; Nature by the uneducated farmer whose parentage is in doubt, Stephen Wonham. Ansell and Wonham when they meet combine forces to win Rickie over to Reality. Rickie is held back by forces in himself and by other characters who though less important represent Sawston more fully. The theme of the book is the struggle to win the Sawstonian Rickie over to real feeling, real thought, real activity; to destroy spurious sentiment. It is a rich book. Mr. Forster himself thinks it is his best, perhaps because it is clearly the most personal. Although Rickie dies in the end, and we must not identify him with Mr. Forster, Rickie is a kind of self-projection by the author :

as if the author were saying, ' There, but for the grace
of God, go I.'   There is much else in the book, but
this confrontation of Sawston and its values is the core,
as it is in the first book.   And again the struggle for
salvation—it is no less—is only partially successful.
Once more, too, for those who fail to be saved, or who
are, from the first, incapable of salvation, there is no
pity; as, on the other hand, there is no punishment.
The damned are quite happy.

In *The Longest Journey* appears for the first time a
character who in various re-incarnations has an important place in all the later novels.   It is characteristic
that she is dead.   She is Rickie's mother, Mrs. Eliot.
She has an inner spiritual beauty, and is incapable of
managing external affairs efficiently, but she is loved
by all good and true people and by social inferiors.
And her ' presence ' broods over the book; her influence, though she is dead, works through the lives of the
living, and if properly understood, works for good.
With her must be associated her brother, Rickie's uncle,
Mr. Failing, also dead.   He is her male counterpart,
and shares her characteristics, though without a close
personal relationship to Rickie.

The next novel, *A Room with a View*, repeats the basic
theme.   It is again Italy, and Nature in both England
and Italy, against Sawston.   As in both the earlier
books, there is a fight between Sawston and its opponents for the soul of the chief character, though this
time the chief character is a girl, Lucy.   This time
the forces of life triumph over the forces of death; true
love of the arts, of fields and woods and mountains,

genuine sexual love, and atheism, triumph over pseudo-culture, stuffy rooms, virginity and Christianity. We are not told that the forces of death vote Conservative, but certainly the forces of life vote, or would vote if they could, socialist. So although this is in appearance a slight and simple novel, we may see the theme broadening out to include, by implication at least, many of the burning questions of the day.

A Room with a View also includes a mother-figure. In *The Longest Journey* the mother-figure is shadowy and composite; it is made up of both Mrs. Elliot, the actual dead mother of the hero, and of Mr. Failing his dead uncle. In *A Room with a View* the mother-figure is single and alive, but this time in the guise of a father, Mr. Emerson, whose tenderness for his son can only be called maternal. He is entirely good, almost a saint, quite without cant, powerfully socialist and atheist, wise, and gifted with deep intuitive insight into the workings of the heart. It is through his agency that the heroine is saved from the horrors of suburbia, virginity, and Christianity.

These three novels I have mentioned, for all their attractive charm and humour, their subtlety and hinted depths, are not the basis of Mr. Forster's unquestioned claim to greatness as a novelist. This claim (which Mr. Forster could never be thought arrogant enough to make for himself!) rests on *Howards End* and *A Passage to India*, which are in a clear line of development from the earlier novels, but which easily transcend them in nearly all their virtues.

With *Howards End* we return to the purely English

scene. Once again Sawston is confronted, but the
conflicts are subtler and wider-reaching in their implications. Schematization here demands more simplification than it did in the earlier novels, because the
novelist's view is more subtle. However, it is still true
to say that Sawston is opposed by Nature. Nature is
still the old pastoral England, which is for Mr. Forster
the true, essential, yeoman England ; and this Nature,
which is England, is symbolised by the house, Howards
End, and the last patch of ground left belonging to it
from a once larger estate. (It is characteristic of the
older English view of nature that nature can be symbolised by an old farmhouse, an old elm-tree, a bit of
lawn, a big hedge, and a small meadow.) Nature,
England (they are here the same) is still, by and through
its symbol, Howards End, a source of strength, of the
good life ; we hear of the binding power of earth.
Nature is represented as victorious at the end of the
book, but the victory is a little unconvincing, and we
feel strongly in places that it is Nature, England, herself
who is in danger ; in danger from commercialism and
mechanisation at the hands of Sawston. Sawston is seen
in this novel more in its public aspect. In the earlier
novels the men who provide the money for Sawston's
widows and virgins to go on trips to Italy are out of
sight, but in *Howards End* the men, and the strong
positive tone they bring to Sawston, are very much to
the fore as managers, business men, administrators ; and
as the sources of the decisions that govern family life.
Sawston is presented as more powerful, more worthy of
respect, and more dangerous. Sawston is as usual cut

off from a true feeling for Nature, and thus for England.
It is therefore in the process of destroying England
physically with cheap building and the motor-car; in
the novel also by its handling of the house Howards
End. It is destroying England spiritually within its
own individuals (who are after all English), and in its
treatment of other non-Sawstonian English, by a stupid
incapacity for love, and by a muddled incoherence of
feeling which refuses to recognise the importance of
feeling at all. Sawston is summed up in the book as
the ' outer life ', the ' life of telegrams and anger ', the
life of prose.

The struggle against Sawston is as much on behalf
of Nature as carried on by Nature. The chief op-
ponent of Sawston, the ' outer life ', is the ' inner life ',
the life of passion, love and affection, personal relations;
the life too, of the mind, the disinterested search for the
true and beautiful; culture in Arnold's sense of the
word. The inner life is a fuller, warmer version of
the life represented by the Cambridge of *The Longest
Journey*. The outer life is the life of the Wilcox family.
The competence in affairs of Henry Wilcox, the heavy,
ruthless, successful business man is the outer case of
a personal inner life which is shabby, muddled and
disregarded. His two grown-up sons are much the
same as he, but coarser, more brutal, and less successful.
Mrs. Wilcox is an exception, to whom I shall return
later. The inner life is the life of the two young Schlegel
sisters, Margaret and Helen, highly educated in both
mind and feelings, sharply self-aware.

In *Howards End* the conflict between Sawston and its

old opponents is still the theme, but the theme is complicated in especial by two developments. Mr. Forster
in this book, as never before, recognises the virtues of
the outer life and the weaknesses of the inner life, and
he entangles the two opponents, outer life and inner
life, as he does not in the earlier books. The entangle-
ment is shown in terms of plot by the personal and family
relationships of the characters on each side. He de-
cides, and causes his characters, especially Margaret
Schlegel, to recognise, that without the Wilcox success
in running affairs, in making money, there would be
little opportunity for the inner life to exist at all: there
would be no money, hence no leisure, hence no culture.
On the other hand, he represents the inner life as
positively inefficient in managing the practical affairs
which keep people alive. If the representatives of the
inner life do anything at all, they manage farms; and
the farms go to ruin. The inner life cannot exist on its
own: it would starve. So the chief necessity is for
reconciliation between Sawston and its opponents.
The book presents the conflict, and also presents a plea
for its cessation, so that the strength of one side may
supplement the weakness of the other. The two must
be connected: in the book's own well-known phrases,
' only connect '; ' connect the prose and the passion '.
Let the inner life bring to the outer warmth and an
ordered, honest passion. Let the outer life, filled now
with a feeling for truth and beauty, manage the inner
life's estates properly. The union is brought about in
the book by the marriage of Margaret Schlegel with Mr.
Wilcox, after the death of the first Mrs. Wilcox.

The conflict then, between Sawston and its opponents, which has occupied the earlier novels and part of *Howards End*, seems to have been brought to a satisfactory conclusion. Neither side is the victor, and each now may strengthen the other. But in fact, the conflict has not been truly ended. The ending of the novel is a little contrived, and in comparison with the solidity of the earlier parts, is blurred a little in the rosy glow of wishfulfillment.

What has happened is that the essential conflict has not so much ceased as retreated further back, on to a different plane. There is a famous passage early in *Howards End* where the two Schlegel sisters are listening to Beethoven's Fifth Symphony. Helen makes a sort of myth of it; she feels that in the third movement Beethoven describes the coming of terrible goblins; they bring terror because they 'merely observed in passing that there was no such thing as splendour or heroism in the world . . . but only panic and emptiness' (Chapter V). Panic and emptiness are precisely what lie behind the Wilcox's worldly efficiency (cf. Chapter III). Later, Margaret hears a 'goblin footfall', when Mrs. Bast has risen to visit her out of the abyss of poverty 'telling of a life where love and hatred had both decayed' (Chapter XIII). This is a kind of metaphysical fear: it is the natural fear of a conclusion which would seem to be inescapable for an atheist, that the world, that human effort, that all the values of the inner life, have absolutely no significance. If there is no God, if death is the end of all, what can anything really matter, apart from getting as much happiness out of life as one can? But the goblins are not unopposed, though the opposition is indirect. Set against the intuition of meaninglessness, and its consequent panic and emptiness, is another intuition of opposite intent. There is the love of England, ' connecting on this side with the joys of the flesh, and on that with the inconceivable ' (Chapter XXIV). And associated with this there comes to the miserable Leonard Bast, a little while before his death on a lovely morning in the country, ' the conviction of innate goodness elsewhere. It was not the optimism he had been taught at school. Again and again must the drums tap, the goblins stalk over the universe, before joy can be purged of the superficial. It was rather paradoxical and rose from his sorrow ' (Chapter XLI).

The association between this conflict of views about the nature of the universe and the smaller conflict between Sawston and its opponents is very close. Sawston, through the Wilcoxes, is associated with fundamental panic and emptiness: Nature connects with ' the inconceivable ', with ' innate goodness elsewhere ', and whatever these may be, they are clearly of the same metaphysical quality as, though hostile to, the goblins. What has happened is the generalisation of the hateful and evil qualities of Sawston into something universal. Curiously, it is this generalisation which makes the representations of Sawston more tolerable. Sawston is dwarfed under a larger horror, and so becomes less menacing in itself, and its virtues may be seen. Similarly the opponents of Sawston, sheltering under the inconceivable innate goodness, may be looked at a little more

dispassionately, for in the emergence of the great principles the actors are less important and more fully human.

The emergence of these great principles is one of the
sources of greatness in the book, for without any straining after effect, without any crude division into good
and evil, the implications of the story go wider and wider.
One of the themes of the book is the relation of the seen
to the unseen. It is only the positive principle which
is denoted by the ' unseen ', only ' innate goodness '.
For the essence of the goblins, once the nursery-my-
thology is left aside, is that they mean negation, of
heroism, of splendour, of life itself; the goblins are
not the unseen, they are *nothing*, and hence horror. The
connexion between the seen and the unseen is made
chiefly by Mrs. Wilcox, who dies quite early in the
book, but whose influence is active throughout the rest
of the book ; and by Margaret Schlegel. When Margaret
was a child of thirteen she ' had grasped a dilemma that
most people travel through life without perceiving . . .
Her conclusion was that any human being lies nearer
to the unseen than any organization ' (Chapter IV).
Mrs. Wilcox is the person who of all persons is near to
the unseen.

> She was not intellectual, nor even alert, and it was odd
> that, all the same, she should give the idea of greatness.
> . . . There was no bitterness in Mrs. Wilcox; there was
> not even criticism ; she was lovable, and no ungracious
> or uncharitable word had passed her lips. Yet she and
> daily life were out of focus : one or the other must show
> blurred. And at lunch she seemed more out of focus
> than usual, and nearer the line that divides daily life from

a life that may be of greater importance.

(Chapter IX)

The tentativeness of that last sentence is very characteristic of Mr. Forster. Mrs. Wilcox undoubtedly is
one of Mr. Forster's saints. It must also be said that
this is a very Sawstonian and sentimental idea of saintliness. There seems no historical basis for saying that
saints (of whatever persuasion) are necessarily inefficient
in daily life; some are, some are not, like the rest
of us. The gap between daily life and the other life
that may be of importance is again characteristic of
late nineteenth-century English religious belief which
set Sunday—and sometimes Sunday's beliefs—so far
apart from other days.

Mrs. Wilson loves England, and loves Howards End
that is a symbol of the old true England; and it is
clearly stated by Margaret that Mrs. Wilcox and
England work to bring things to a good end. Margaret
says that she feels that all the persons in the story, and
even the house with its tree, are only fragments of Mrs.
Wilcox's mind, even after death (Chapter XL). Of
course Mr. Forster himself is not committed literally
to such a belief. But Margaret is very much a mouth-
piece of the author. And Mr. Forster certainly seems
to have this strange belief in some persons' survival
after death, if the typically vague sentence at the end
of *The Hill of Devi* means what it seems to mean.

Mrs. Wilcox is a mystical mother, holding up her
chosen ones in this life from beyond the grave. It is
interesting that she is so remote from the children of
her blood. Few are called, and fewer still are chosen

to be hers, and none of them are her own children.

In *Howards End* the mystical mother, the Earth-mother, as we may call her from her relation to England and Nature, who haunts in various shape some of the earlier books and short stories, has fully come forth. She is Reality, as sought by Cambridge, she is Nature, who seeks the good characters of the Italy books ; she is the enemy of the superficial, of false sentiment ; she is innate goodness. What her relation to the goblins is, we do not know, but we have a sense, or we are meant to have a sense, that she triumphs over them. This is the most optimistic of Mr. Forster's books. If England to herself be true, come all the goblins of the world and we shall shock them.

In Mr. Forster's next and last novel, *A Passage to India*, the mystic mother becomes even more dominant and important, but her relation to the deeper metaphysical implications alters. In *Howards End* the mystical mother is very closely associated with the old, true England, that is, for Mr. Forster, Nature. And in the earlier books and short stories Nature is a power which, rightly understood, fosters and supports the chosen few of mankind, even though Nature has also terror. As I have remarked in the previous essay, Nature in Europe came to be regarded as the deputy of God ; and as Mr. Forster conceives Pan, the Greek divinity who embodies the forces of nature, he may be capricious, strange, to Sawston obscene and terrifying (as in the short *Story of a Panic*), but he is divine, a source of life, joy, true feeling. This concept is deep-rooted in European literature. It would be possible to show important

similarities between Chaucer's Nature (and the sources
he drew on) and Mr. Forster's Pan.   But such a concept is hardly possible in India.

Most of the inhabitants of India do not mind how
India is governed.   Nor are the lower animals of England
concerned about England, but in the tropics the indifference is more prominent, the inarticulate world is closer
at hand and readier to resume control as soon as men are
tired. . . . April, herald of horrors was at hand.   The sun
was returning to his kingdom with power but without
beauty—that was the sinister feature.   If only there had
been beauty! His cruelty would have been tolerable then.
Through excess of light he failed to triumph, he also;
in his yellowy-white overflow not only matter, but brightness itself lay drowned.   He was not the unattainable
friend, either of men or birds or other suns, he was not
the eternal promise, the never-withdrawn suggestion that
haunts our consciousness; he was merely a creature, like
the rest, and so debarred from glory.

(A Passage to India, Chapter 10)

Nature is indifferent to man and all his values.   This
is the worst horror, just as it is the worst horror of the
goblins in *Howards End* that they are indifferent.

This indifference exacerbates the conflict which is
within the plot of *A Passage to India,* for nature's indifference becomes hateful inconvenience to the conditions of human life.   Men are crushed by the sun,
and the more irritable with each other.

At the centre of the book is again Sawston; this time
transplanted to India, and as a consequence more essentially Sawstonian than ever.   We see Sawston again
in its more public aspect, its men not this time business

men, but administrators of Empire. Because of local
conditions, and because they are cut off from the general
life of England with all its subtle checks and balances,
they live, more than they could in England, by the
ideals of the late nineteenth-century minor public
school—ideals which Mr. Forster very reasonably, to
judge from his presentation of them, regards with profound dislike. He gives Sawston its due, as he sees it. He
praises the incorruptible honesty, the energy, the concern
with order.   But he also shows very clearly the panic and
emptiness which lie within, and which subtly corrupt
even the virtues.   Thus, when Ronny the magistrate has
spoken eloquently to his mother of his duty to India,

> He spoke sincerely, but she could have wished with less
> gusto. How Ronny revelled in the drawbacks of his
> situation.   How he did rub it in that he was not in India
> to behave pleasantly, and derived positive satisfaction
> therefrom ! *He reminded her of his public-schooldays.*   The
> traces of young-man humanitarianism had sloughed off,
> and he talked like an intelligent and embittered boy.   His
> words without his voice might have impressed her, but
> when she heard the self-satisfied lilt of them, when she
> saw the mouth moving so complacently and competently
> beneath the little red nose, she felt, quite illogically, that
> this was not the last word on India.   One touch of regret
> —not the canny substitute *but the true regret from the heart*
> —would have made him a different man, and the British
> Empire a different institution.
>
>   (Chapter V.   *Italics mine.*)

The theme of the novel is the conflict of Sawston of
the undeveloped heart against a civilisation where the
heart's affections find their true place.   This is the same

as the conflict in *Howards End* between the outer life
and the inner. And again the inner life, that is, in the
latter book, Indian culture (whether Hindu or Moslem)
is shown as lacking the practical virtues of the outer. It
is the same as the conflict in the earlier novels, between
Sawston and Nature, Sawston and Italy.

As In *Howards End*, though much more tentatively,
a reconciliation between the two opposing elements is
shown to be possible. Fielding the Englishman, though
a solitary figure, throws his lot in with the Indians, and
his best friend is Aziz the Moslem doctor. But a more
important person, Mrs. Moore, also understand Indians,
and understands more than Fielding. Mrs. Moore is
Mrs. Wilcox again, the mystical mother. She has little
feeling for her Sawstonian son Ronny. While alive
she achieves nothing. She is great in being, not in
doing. She departs and dies long before the end of the
book. But in some strange way, as with Mrs. Wilcox,
her influence after death is stronger than in life, and
works for good. In the crisis of the novel, when Adela
tells the truth in the great court-scene, we are led to
feel vaguely but strongly that it is Mrs. Moore's good
influence that has prevailed. And in the strange and
moving religious festival at the end of the book there is
a mysterious connexion established between her and the
high priest.

But the presentation of Mrs. Moore is in several ways
more complex than that of Mrs. Wilcox. For one thing,
it is Mrs. Moore, and no other character on either side
of the conflict, who has suffered the terrifying vision of
nullity, of the meaningless, valueless, quality of life,

which is suggested more faintly by the goblins of
Howards End. Her vision is conveyed in that great
and poetical passage which describes her awful experience
in the Marabar caves. This total negation of all the
worth in human life crushes Mrs. Moore. She loses
her earlier Christian faith and becomes a fretful selfish
old woman. When she dies on her way home it is
apparently in deep cynicism.

Here we must recall the fainter yet obviously identical
vision of nullity in *Howards End*. The vision can only
come to anti-Sawston characters, to Margaret and Helen
Schlegel, to Mrs. Moore. Yet it is a vision of what
seriously lies at the back of Sawston, panic and emptiness. The vision of the Marabar caves is a vision of
the empty heart of Sawston. Marabar is all that Mr.
Forster hates in the society of his choice.

And just as in *Howards End* the complete nullity
suggested by the goblins was offset by the ' innate
goodness elsewhere ' represented by Mrs. Wilcox, so
in *A Passage to India* there is something set against the
Marabar experience. It lies partly the enduring influence of Mrs. Moore as seen in Adela's long struggle
with herself, and in the mystical connexion of Mrs.
Moore with the high priest of the religious festival.
The Marabar is also contrasted with another vision,
much less impressive, of Mrs. Moore's, when on her
journey home across India she glimpses a place called
Asirgarh ;

it had huge and noble bastions and to the right of them
was a mosque. She forgot it. Ten minutes later, Asirgarh reappeared. . . . What could she connect it with

except its own name? Nothing; she knew no one who lived there. But it had looked at her twice and seemed to say: 'I do not vanish'. . . . 'I have not seen the right places,' she thought . . . presently the boat sailed and thousands of coconut palms appeared all round the anchorage, and climbed the hills to wave her farewell. 'So you thought an echo was India; you took the Marabar caves as final?' they laughed. 'What have we in common with them, or they with Asirgarh? Goodbye!'

(Chapter XXIII)

Asirgarh and all the variety of India in a way mock Marabar. Sawston once more is confronted by a vision of life.

Mr. Forster himself has recently made an interesting comment on the vision of the Marabar in an interview with Mr. Angus Wilson. They had been discussing the 'idea of momentary vision', presumably such visions as that I have quoted of Asirgarh, or that experienced by Leonard Bast on the morning he died. Of the vision in the Marabar Mr. Forster commented,

It's a moment of negation. I suppose it's the same thing as the vision we have discussed with its back turned.
(*Encounter*, November 1957, p. 54)

Marabar is the vision of goodness with its back turned. We may justifiably take a leap of the imagination and say that in the same way Sawston itself is a negation of something positive, rather than something positive itself. In other words, both Sawston and anti-Sawston are aspects of the same fundamental unity. This accounts for the desire to reconcile Sawston and anti-Sawston in the last two books. Even more, it gives us grounds

for wondering if the antipathy to Sawston is quite what
it has always seemed to be.

When we look back over the novels we are bound to
be impressed by the general similarity of pattern in
them. Although the novels become much richer and
denser in technique and content, it is remarkable how
consistent is the novelist's attitude throughout his work.
The general theme is the same. Actual persons in one
novel are mentioned casually in another (like Miss
Quested). Key-figures and key-phrases are repeated.
The mother-figure is the chief recurring character, but
there are others. Margaret Schlegel is rather similar
to Stewart Ansell, and Agnes' tragedy in *The Longest
Journey* is that that ' inner life ' is withdrawn from
her which is so much a subject of consideration in
Howards End. The unity of impression, with all their
rich variety, that the novels make, is rather remarkable.
The subject is always Sawston, and, we realise more and
more, is *only* Sawston. Mr. Forster is obsessed with
Sawston, and incapable of escaping from Sawston.
When we consider all this, and the hint given about the
Marabar Caves, and look at his attitudes more closely,
we are bound to conclude that he himself is as Sawstonian, at bottom, as any of his most disliked characters.
He condemns Herbert Pembroke in *The Longest Journey*
for his sole interest in success, either worldly or spiritual.
But is the novelist himself concerned with anything else ?
(I leave aside the question whether he would be sensible
to be concerned with anything else.) Is there any character who shows us the virtue of failure ? The only full-
scale portrait of complete failure is Leonard Bast, and he,

in so far as he commands our belief, only draws our pity.
In so far as Rickie fails he is condemned, if with some pity.
The novelist's idea of success is naturally more subtle
than that of such characters as Herbert Pembroke who is
' stupid ' : or rather, the novelist's view is more far-
sighted than that of such characters ; but it looks in
the same direction. Thus Mr. Failing was a failure
as a farmer, but one is left in no doubt that his practice
would ultimately have led to better farming. The
novelist, like a true practical Sawstonian (practicality is
the great Sawston virtue) values the earth for what it
can give him, not for itself. He is like an employer
who treats his men well because that is how he can get
the best out of them. The novelist differs from his
Sawston kindred in being more, not less, practical.
' " How unpractical it all is ! " That was [Ansell's]
comment on Dunwood House. " How unbusiness-like !
They live together without love." ' The association
between business and love gives business the primacy,
and Ansell's opinions are clearly those of the novelist
himself. Mr. Trilling in his valuable book to which
this essay and all who value Mr. Forster's works are so
much indebted, quotes D. H. Lawrence's remark that
Mr. Forster made ' a nearly deadly mistake glorifying
those *business* people in *Howards End*. Business is no
good.' Mr. Trilling comments that Lawrence was
here ' indulging his taste for the unconditional. It
led him to read Forster inaccurately and it led him to
make that significant shift from " business people " to
" business ".' (*E. M. Forster*, p. 18). But in fact
Lawrence is here seeing deeply into the essential nature

of Mr. Forster's Sawstonian outlook. At bottom Mr. Forster does glorify ' business ', though he condemns many business-men for being so unbusiness-like as to live without love. Mr. Trilling is equally mistaken, I think, in seeing *Howards End* as one of " the great comments on the class struggle ". There is only one class in the novels, the middle-class; to which Sawston is related as the cream is to the milk. Leonard Bast is in the same class as the Schlegels, though only just clinging to the edge of it, terrified lest he fall off into the abyss of poverty where those live who do not ' pretend to be gentlefolk '. Wherever one looks, one sees that the novelist's wishes are those of Sawston. He does not condemn the British Empire. He sees that it is being lost in India for want of a smile. He sees, that is, how unbusiness-like it is to run an Empire without love. But like any Sawstonian imperialist he wants to run the Empire. It is the same with culture. In the earlier books he smiles at the false culture of Sawston. Culture is the hall-mark of gentility. Yet in a brief comment in *Howards End* (Chapter XXXI) he praises the Schlegel's house ' which had never mistaken culture for an end.' How very Sawstonian to think that culture must be justified by having an end beyond itself, must have a use besides a value.

This unconscious allegiance to what is condemned in the books leads to serious limitations in the picture of the world which all great art must claim to show. Take the question of virginity and infertility. In essence Mr. Forster condemns Sawston for infertility, but presents as a desirable alternative a world equally infertile.

This is a limitation in both ways. An inadequate condemnation of virginity on the one hand : an inadequate presentation of fertility on the other. The chief scapegoat of virginity is Mr. Beebe at the end of *A Room with a View* who at the end of the book takes a rather unconvincing turn to the sinister with his belief in celibacy. Truly, Sawston itself is blighted, the women infertile. Agnes, and Lilia (in *Where Angels Fear to Tread*), have babies, but both babies die—Lilia's directly because of Sawston's meddling, unloving, interference. But the good characters do not do much better. There are a few children in the background, very vague. But of the important characters, Philip and Caroline in *Where Angels Fear to Tread* cannot even bring themselves to marry, Rickie is unsuited to marriage, Ansell speaks against it, Margaret Schlegel does not like babies and is glad she has none ; Fielding a man in his forties only at the end manages to marry. Helen Schlegel has the only successful baby, got in a single loveless act of Quixotic self-sacrifice on her part. And this baby belongs to the ending which is generally felt to be a wish-fulfillment, that Howards End, and implicitly England's earth, will be inherited by Mr. Forster's equivalent for the meek ; the lower middle-class.

The essentially Sawstonian quality of the novelist's attitude is now revealed in the dominant figure of the mystic mother. Her Sawstonian quality can be illustrated in two ways : first the way in which she represents a Sawstonian concept, and second, the way in which she is entangled with the Sawstonian image. She represents a Sawstonian concept of the ideal, a kind of secularised saintliness, in her impracticality, in her power to influence people—in fact, her power *over* people—in her inner beauty, and even in her lack of taste (the novelist's double attitude towards ' taste ' is similar to the ambivalence in his attitude to Empire, Nature, culture, religion, and other matters).   I am speaking, for the sake of brevity, of a composite mother-figure : in the actual characters now one trait is dominant, now another. Secondly, she is deeply entangled with the characters of Sawston.   The most disagreeable of them are her husbands and sons, and she shares their opinions.   Mrs. Wilcox gives the clearest example by her remarks at the end of Margaret Schlegel's distressing lunchparty, when she asserts the Wilcox view of the practical value of ' bricks and mortar ', and departs saying memorably, ' But we are all in the same boat, old and young.   I never forget that ' (Chapter IX).   It is clear enough that Sawston and the mystic mother are very closely connected.

Now however deeply committed a Sawstonian the novelist is, he has obviously a deeply divided attitude to Sawston, an attitude of love and dislike, in which on the surface at least, dislike predominates.   We are now not surprised to notice that in just the same way, though much less obviously, he has a deeply divided attitude to the mother-figure, an attitude of love and dislike, in which, this time, love predominates.   This divided attitude is important because it tends to limit the effectiveness of the symbol, and the symbolical significance of Mrs. Wilcox and Mrs. Moore is deliberate and important. If we turn to the consideration of the mother-figure again we cannot but note some singularities. There can be no doubt of the novelist's opinion of the goodness and greatness of Mrs. Wilcox and Mrs. Moore, nor of Rickie's veneration for his mother. Yet the novelist also deliberately presents Mrs. Wilcox and Mrs. Moore as rather boring and rather ' difficult '. There is no doubt that to their social acquaintances and especially to their sons, they are a little tiresome. The extreme example is Vashti in the early short story *The Machine Stops*. They are also either widows or cut off in sympathy from their husbands, and one cannot altogether blame the husbands. As wives and mothers they seem bloodless and curiously infertile (like nearly all Forster's women). Of course they are old, but that so important a figure should be an *old* woman is itself significant of infertility. They are cut off from the sons of their blood, and this is a matter of strong implicit reproach with both Mrs. Elliot and Vashti. It is accepted without complaint in the later novels. Mrs. Moore's younger son Ralph is supposed to have something of her quality, but he is a slight character, and we never see them together, and no point is made of their actual human relationship. It is also very notable that the mothers become much more agreeable, as it were, and much more active in influence, and even helpful, once they are safely dead, and thus even more personally remote than in life. And yet the three major novels, *The Longest Journey*, *Howards End*, *A Passage to India*, are full of mother-worship, for which the justification is not very apparent. A very good image of the whole process is given, in a remarkably detached way, by Rickie's attitude to his mother. The deformed little Rickie was first (rather against psychological probability, perhaps) neglected by his mother, and cruelly teased and neglected by his father (fathers are usually absent or unsympathetic in the novels). Then his mother turned to love him, in compensation perhaps for her own neglect by her husband. After her early death Rickie adores and sentimentalizes her memory. But he hates (at least at first) her 're-incarnation' in the person of his half-brother, Stephen Wonham. One could argue that Rickie's attitude is present, in a different way, throughout the later books, in their whole presentation of the mother-figure. She is adored, and yet there is a vein of suppressed and possibly unrecognised hostility. The same deep division is present in the attitude to Sawston, except that there we have conscious hostility and suppressed, possibly unconscious, love. The mother-figure and Sawston, looked at from this point of view, are complementary figures, closely connected. It is arguable, indeed, that the veiled love of Sawston is an expression of the love felt for the mother-image.

The veiled hostility to the mother-image spreads to all the women in the books, and also to the presentation of marriage, and to parent-child relationships. How implacably the novelist pursues Mrs. Herriton, Agnes, Charlotte, Dolly, Mrs. Turton, and their associates. He mildly approves, or at least does not feel strongly about those women who are rejected by Sawston for one reason or another, like the vulgar Lilia, the adulter-

ous Miss Derek, the dull but honest Miss Quested.   The
only women he approves of are in a special position,
and are, as it were, the novelist's *personae*, Caroline and
Lucy in the early novels, and the Schlegel sisters.
Helen is the most vividly realised, but they are all rather
sexless creatures—flattened figures! The Sawstonian
women are more disagreeable than the men, and the
Collector in *A Passage to India* is made to say 'After all,
it's our women who make everything more difficult out
here' (Chapter 24).   They make the men worse,
more Sawstonian.

There is a dearth of ordinary marriages in the books,
full as they are of widows and virgins.   (I should make
it clear that here, as everywhere else in this essay, I
am not concerned with Mr. Forster's *personal* opinions.
As to his personal opinion of marriage, it is high, as he
himself has recently said in *Encounter*, November 1957,
and *The London Magazine*, November 1957.   I am only
concerned with the shape of his artistic imagination.) The
only love-affair between young people is the bloodless
romance between George and Lucy in *A Room with a
View*, where interestingly enough the infertile mother-
image has been temporarily metamorphosed into the
only tender father, Mr. Emerson.   Were it not for
Mr. Emerson, neither of the principals could have been
brought together in marriage.   The marriages of Margaret and Stephen in other books are the results of theses,
of ideas about what ought to happen, or about what is
desirable.   And indeed in *A Passage to India* Mrs.
Moore says 'Why all this marriage, marriage? . . .
The human race would have become a single person

centuries ago if marriage was any use. And all this rubbish about love . . . ' (Chapter 22). This is a dramatic comment, not the novelist's own : and yet it is true of the trend of his artistic imagination.

There is equally a dearth of parent-child relationships, obviously connected with the unsatisfactory nature of the mother-figure and other women. It is again to be noted that the only book in which what we may call a normal pattern of human relationships is attempted is *A Room with a View*, where George and Lucy fall in love and are married ; where each has a satisfactory relationship with a parent, Lucy to her widowed mother, George to his widowed father ; and where the form of the dominant mother-symbol is a father. The only other satisfactory child-parent relationship in the books that is made anything of, is Stewart Ansell's relationship to that very shadowy though pleasant figure, his father—his father, be it noted, not his mother. Other children are orphans or out of sympathy with their parents. This again is not in accord with what seem to be the novelist's *opinions* (here expressed in the books through character and action). Stephen Wonham is shown at the end loving his child, as he was loved by Mr. Failing his uncle— both ideal figures and unconvincing imaginatively. Much is made, with profound insight, of Gino's love for his baby son, but the baby is killed by Sawstonian interference. Gino, however, is another ideal character, and moreover an Italian. Even in these ideal cases, however, there is no parent-child relationship actually presented. What is interesting, too, is that in these

ideal parent-child patterns, which are never developed,
it is always a father, never a mother. And the ideal
young fathers contrast very strongly with the imaginatively better realised old fathers, from Mr. Elliot onwards, who are disagreeable or unsympathetic. The
failure of the mother-image to be a real mother is perhaps reflected in the wish-fulfillment affection of the
young fathers. The only fairly motherly woman is
Helen Schlegel, who only becomes a mother right at
the end of the book, so that no developing relationship
between her and the child is possible. She is, moreover, the mother of an illegitimate child, and only appears as a mother in the rather forced ending of *Howards
End*.

There is a relative failure in the portrayals of the
mother-image, of marriage, of parent-child relationship.
It is relative because Mr. Forster still remains, for any
limitations to be pointed out in mapping the shape of
his imaginative world, a great novelist. It is failure
because the shaping imagination does not in these cases
respond to the calls made on it by the conscious guiding
will. In particular one is bound to feel that the mother-
image fails to be an adequate record of, or response to,
experience of the nature of the world. Too much is
expected of her, especially in *Howards End*. She should
be a goddess, and though we may suspend our disbelief in her while under the immediate magic of the
novel, she fails to impose herself finally on our imaginations when we are asked to feel her workings after
death. Mrs. Moore is a more vividly realised character than Mrs. Wilcox, her *post mortem* influence more

subtly and effectively portrayed, but it is still difficult
to respond to the mystical quality of her existence,
difficult to respond to her greatness. Perhaps in another kind of book one might have been persuaded that
she ' worked ' after her death, like a saint, performing
the modern equivalents of miracles of healing. But
in the books as they are, so naturalistic, so materialistic,
it is difficult to feel that in total, alive and dead, the
mother-figure corresponds to reality, rather than to
wishful thinking.

There are other limitations in the books, which derive
from this limitation in the dominant symbol of the
mother. For all his emphasis on personal relations,
especially in *Howards End*, the novels are not very illuminating about them ; the true subject is the failure
of personal relations. The novelist makes a significant
comment describing Mrs. Moore's feelings about India :

> She felt increasingly (vision or nightmare ?) that though
> people are important, the relations between them are
> not, and that in particular too much fuss has been made
> over marriage ; centuries of carnal embracement, yet man
> is no nearer to understanding man.
>
> (Chapter 14)

This brief passage, like so much of Mr. Forster's
writing, is like the centre of a spider's web ; it sends out
threads of intelligent delicate suggestion in a number
of directions. The point it so clearly makes here is
only one of the significances. Like the remark quoted
earlier which is made about Mrs. Moore's opinion of
marriage, it is a dramatic comment, not necessarily the

novelist's own ; but it sufficiently indicates the trend of the artistic imagination.

There are other limitations in the novels, for example a limitation in the knowledge of the inner life of the characters, which taken in conjunction with the emphasis on the inner life, must also be called a weakness, if not a failure. Much less important is the narrow range of characters and the lack of suggestion of other types of character and occupation. But limitation, rather than weakness or failure is the best word for all these short-comings. In a lesser novelist one would have expected to find some warping under the weight of this strangely limited mother-figure. Yet it is not so. The books are more limited in their scope than they first appear, but the imagination is not seriously warped.

We may sum up these limitations as characteristically the limitations of Sawston, or as characteristically the limitations of the mother-figure. In the last analysis the two are to be identified, Sawston as the general aspect, the mother-figure as the more personal aspect. Together they constitute the total ' objective correlative ' which is the body of Mr. Forster's imaginative work ; they constitute the total imaginative concept with which he is obsessed. Part of the greatness of Mr. Forster as a novelist is the richness and intricacy with which the concept is traced, the relations within it of one part to another, and the deep interest which it arouses as a microcosm of experience. It is Mr. Forster's personal ' convention ', in the sense developed in the first essay in this book, by which he takes hold of experience, or reflects experience. Much of the strength of the con-

vention is derived from the same source that limits it
in the directions I have indicated; the deeply divided
nature of his attitude, the complicated mixture of love
and dislike with which he beholds and presents it.   His
divided attitude to almost all matters of experience and
belief is the most typical single characteristic of all Mr.
Forster's work.   It is not that, in the most modern
jargon, he is not ' committed ' : he is committed to two
inconsistent things, to the goblins and to innate goodness, to Marabar and Asirgarh ; and he is passionately
committed to both.   He says in an essay on *What I
believe* that he does not believe in belief.   He might have
said equally well that he firmly believes in not believing.
This double attitude may be logically difficult to defend,
but I suspect that it is also difficult to attack logically.
Everywhere in Mr. Forster's imaginative work we find
the *pro* and the *contra*.   It occurs on a small scale in
his sentences, and could be illustrated from several of
the quotations I have already made for other purposes,
just as it forms the general structure of his imagination.   He presents everything as ambivalent.   What
he says of Rickie might equally well be applied to
himself :

> For Rickie suffered from the Primal Curse, which is
> not—as the Authorised Version suggests—the knowledge
> of good and evil, but the knowledge of good-and-evil.
> (Chapter XVIII)

In this divided mind, that is only occasionally at odds
with itself, lies all the capacity to see, as so often he
does, the good in the evil and the evil in the good.   It

saves his ideal characters from being absurd and his unpleasant characters from being inhuman. In it is rooted his charity, his wisdom, and also his pervading comedy. In it too is rooted his sensitive feeling for intuition, along with his belief in the practical and the business-like. It makes him tentative, undogmatic, for he is always conscious of an opposite possibility. It allows him to entertain the supernatural in a naturalistic and materialistic world. It makes him at times almost maddeningly elusive. It can lead him astray occasionally into mere whimsicality. It is the source of his refusal to be dignified. It can make him both tender and cruel. I should not say it has made him a great novelist: but it is inseparable to the kind of great novelist he is.

THE MODERN ENGLISH LITERARY
TEMPER AND THE CRISIS OF EXPANSION

This short essay, and this portentous title, go somewhat uneasily together. Yet it would be shirking the
issues raised in previous essays not to say something,
however brief and necessarily inadequate, about the
temper of modern English literature.

Since 1945 there has been a great social revolution
within Great Britain, and a great change in the position
of Great Britain in relation to other countries. To
discuss these changes at all would necessarily be to go
far beyond the possible bounds of this essay, yet they
are the indirect causes of many changes in the general
tone of post-war literature and must be born in mind.
Even so, social revolution and changes in the pattern
of world power since 1945 are naturally products of
causes lying still further back. Although these causes
are no doubt capable of being treated in an almost
infinite regression, it is not really necessary to go back
beyond the nineteenth century for literary purposes.
In that century something really new did come into the
world, however we may trace its causes further back.
The new thing was the birth and astonishing growth,
for the first time in the world's history, of modern
industrialism and modern science, giving rise to the
modern industrial mass society, with its new power,
new material standards, huge new quantities of goods

and of people especially—and consequently with its
demand for new qualities, new standards. This vast
material expansion, and the explosion of new ideas which
was both its cause and effect, gave rise to a crisis of
culture. The astonishing decline in standards of taste
all over nineteenth-century Europe is one of the most
obvious signs. Another is the alienation of the artist
almost everywhere from his society. The necessity for
Arnold's long maintained crusade against the cultural
Philistine is another obvious witness in England. It is
essentially this crisis of culture which is still working
itself out in England; for that there *is* such a crisis,
along with all the other crises that beset us, everyone
is agreed. It is a crisis of expansion. The effect of
continuing success in controlling the forces of nature,
in raising material standards of living; in a word, in
acquiring more power both for society and for individuals
in controlling their own lives, is to bring more and more
people up to the level where they can choose what shall
occupy their minds beyond the absolute necessity of
getting a living for themselves and their families. In
such a case, the subjects of choice are many, though
not unlimited. One may choose to devote himself
simply to higher and higher material standards; another may choose, at the other extreme, to devote himself to the acqusition of the most abstract and apparently
useless knowledge. It would be difficult to do either
completely, and especially to devote oneself only to
increased material goods, because almost nothing is
purely material. Man's capacity for food and drink is
limited. Higher quality must inevitably soon be sub-

stituted for greater quantity once we get above the
subsistence level. More motor-cars soon turn into
better motor-cars, and then arise questions of taste as
well as of performance. More leisure demands that it
be filled with attractive activity, and attractive activity
implies the use of the imagination. The essence of our
crisis of expansion is that more and more people are less
and less trained, or experienced, in imaginative power,
to choose satisfactory attractive activities. It is at
bottom an educational crisis.

The function of education is to prepare us for handling
experience. A bad education is one which is inadequate
or false to the experiences which do or will confront us.
In this sense one may say that the education of an il-
literate tribesman in a static primitive society untouched
by distorting outside influences, is likely, if that society
has existed for some time, to be a good education. It
has fitted him to deal with the experiences he will have
met, though such an education would not fit him for
other societies, or for striking developments in his own.
It is probably true to say that for all the appalling misery
and suffering of pre-nineteenth century England, for
all the many things wrong with society, most of its
members, high or low, were tolerably well educated,
(except in the London slums) even if they could not read
or write. But in the nineteenth century the conditions
of life changed so sharply and radically that most people,
even when they had the best formal education then
available, were relatively badly educated. This was
especially the case with the enormously expanded
middle-class. The old town and parochial culture was

destroyed, and it is a long process to formulate a new cultural pattern. It is a crisis of expansion because the difficulty is caused by the extra facilities, the wider horizons, continually opening out. Continually more and more knowledge, greater and richer stimulation goad the mind and senses, and we hardly know in which direction to run. Television provides an obvious minor example. In England after 1945 the possession of a television set was until the other day the characteristic mark of what once could be described as a working-class household. A prominent politician, two or three years ago, drew a haunting picture of the miseries of the English poor, some of whom were in danger of being reduced to such a state of insecurity as to be in danger of losing their incompletely-paid-for television sets. To such households it is clear that the television set would bring vastly wider horizons than were open before, and that these might open out on vistas both desirable and undesirable. And it is characteristic of the situation that no one can be quite sure of what is truly desirable.

In such a situation it is obvious that literature, which depends on an educated, that is, a prepared-for, response, is likely to suffer, and is bound to charge. The conventions, deep and superficial, which govern society and literature, are themselves undergoing rapid change. The earliest and best succinct statement of the situation as it affects literature naturally occurs at the beginning of the nineteenth century, equally naturally by a great poet, Wordsworth, whose powers of social and political insight are sometimes neglected. In the 1805 Preface to *The Lyrical Ballads* he writes:

For a multitude of causes, unknown to former times, are now acting with a combined force to blunt the discriminating powers of the mind, and unfitting it for all voluntary exertion to reduce it to a state of almost savage torpor. The most effective of these causes are the great national events which are daily taking place, and the increasing accumulation of men in cities, where the uniformity of their occupations produces a craving for extraordinary incident, which the rapid communication of intelligence hourly gratifies. To this tendency of life and manners the literature and theatrical exhibitions of the country have conformed themselves. The invaluable works of our elder writers, I had almost said the works of Shakespeare and Milton, are driven into neglect by frantic novels, sickly and stupid German Tragedies, and deluges of idle and extravagant stories in verse.—When I think upon this degrading thirst after outrageous stimulation, I am almost ashamed to have spoken of the feeble effort with which I have endeavoured to counteract it . . .

Most later statements of the crisis are unconscious elaborations of this one, and certainly it invites extended comment.

There is one further chief element in the crisis, often pointed to today, but which also arose and was noticed in the nineteenth century. George Eliot says in a letter that her ' sole purpose ' in writing *The Mill on the Floss*

was to show the conflict which is going on everywhere when the younger generation with its higher culture comes into collision with the older.

(To Emily Davis, 21 August 1869)

Since the crisis has always been to some extent recognised

as one to be solved by education, it has always been characteristic that a fairly high proportion of people have received a better formal education (which is roughly what George Eliot here means by ' culture ') than their parents. A more profound view of education might say that children, since the beginning of the nineteenth century, have at any rate had increasingly more *information* than their parents about important modern developments in knowledge, and that consequently their education has been at least different from their parents. In the twentieth century, what adolescent child does not naturally know and feel more than his parents do (special interests apart) about internal combustion engines and space-travel ? In England today, how often a really elderly person is less at ease with a telephone than a five-year-old child. Age is no longer the repository of wisdom, but a wooden vessel stranded by a retreating tide on which the motor-boats scud about. The charts are out of date. And yet the charts—the Tradition— were once good, and there must be a continual effort to revise and re-interpret them. Hence the uneasy attitude to Tradition, the concern with Tradition, or the irritation with Tradition, characteristic of many English writers today. It can neither be taken for granted nor totally ignored. Mr. Eliot's famous essay, *Tradition and the Individual Talent* marks the beginning of self-consciousness about this matter in modern writers. Such self-consciousness, is especially the mark of writers who are attempting to produce work of literary merit, as opposed simply to earning a living by writing. Most of these writers are poets, and this concern tends to set them apart from novelists, who are inclined to worry less about the philosophical or aesthetic basis of their art. The division between poetry and the novel is another characteristic of the crisis of culture, which has also affected our attitude to the entertainment value of the arts.

By entertainment I mean a pleasurable way of passing the time which does not tax our mental or emotional energies too greatly. It is obvious that art, if it is worth anything at all, must do more than entertain. But up to the nineteenth century, most art tended to include within it some element of entertainment (we need not enter the worn-out controversy about the degree to which poetry should teach, or delight). It is typical of the crisis of expansion that it tries to force art to think too much of entertainment—of the gripping story, the happy or the sentimentally sad ending, the avoidance of important but painful topics. The huge mass of new readers in an expanding culture, mostly ill-educated, demands easy excitement. In the nineteenth century, when literature was still the chief imaginative form of entertainment, along with this excitement were often provided higher literary values. In the twentieth century, with new techniques of mass amusement, (cinema, sport, television, produced under enormous commercial pressure,) literature is only one of several kinds of entertainment, and moreover, the simplest literature is more arduous than watching television or films.

The natural response of many serious writers has been to give up the unequal struggle on the field of entertainment. The development is seen most clearly in the writing of verse. Modern verse, unlike earlier English verse, makes little attempt to captivate the reader at first reading. It relies for its appeal on a minority of readers who, for various reasons, are prepared to swallow the pill without the sugar-coating. Hardly any poet nowadays, for example, relies on narrative verse. Yet the pattern of a story can be as subtle a way of conveying meaning as the pattern of a sentence.

The novel has fared both better and worse than poetry. In the hands of most writers entertainment has been the novel's primary aim. It has in consequence been the dominant form of both nineteenth and twentieth century literature, sucking much of the entertainment value from poetry and even from the drama. But as the competition from non-literary forms of entertainment, most of them driven by commercial pressures, has become hotter, so the novel has had to aim more and more at pure entertainment and abandon the attempt to achieve the higher literary values. We can see this process at work in a simple way with the greater and greater streamlining of the novel's form. There is less and less room in the ordinary novel for commentary, description, refinement of feeling. Much of the greatness of Mr. Forster's novels derives from the penetrating commentary which is the warp to the woof of plot and action. For a young writer today so discursive a manner would be impossible. Reflection, refinement and elaboration, if there at all, must be disguised under pseudo-realistic devices.

Nevertheless, in all cases where there is a strong

action there tends to be a strong counter-action. The crisis in culture is being met, however inadequately, by attempts to remedy it; and the remedy is education. It is difficult to know, when all is so close to us that we see every event and tendency through the magnifying glass of our own prejudices, interests and personalities, if things are getting better or worse. But certainly there are some factors which make for a better situation. More people in England are getting a better formal education, and this may mean that they are getting a better education in general. The essence of a crisis of expansion is that wider mental and physical horizons are opened; and where there is more choice, not all men will choose the worse. Even commercial television can on occasion provide something not utterly trivial. While it is impossible to be wholeheartedly optimistic, at least there is still good literature produced in England.

To conclude this essay I shall discuss three modern writers generally felt to be representative of modern English writing, who all derive from the same class, though from slightly different levels; none of them is known to me personally. Each is of certain literary merit, though how much is still a matter of controversy. Each is highly popular in his own field. Two are in their middle thirties, and the other is nearly thirty. I discuss them because their popularity is itself an indication of their representative quality. But I do not claim that any of them is the best contemporary writer in his own field now alive. This essay does not in any way set out to give a full picture of the state of literature in contemporary England ; what are offered are samples and suggestions.

The novelist is of course Kingsley Amis. ' Of course ', because everywhere that there is discussion of post-war literature, there is almost bound to be a reference to *Lucky Jim*, his first novel, published in 1953. The hero, of this book, Jim Dixon, has become an archetype of the post-war young man. Mr. Amis's two later novels have not been so successful. Mr. Amis is the product of a London day-school (of which there is a pleasant account in *The Spectator*, February 28, 1958), war-time service in the Army, and St. John's College, Oxford. He is now a lecturer in English literature in the University of Swansea.

Lucky Jim is an extremely funny book. The essence of the humour is acute and realistic observation of normal minor social embarassments and frustrations, to which is joined fantasy or farce or both. The effect depends on accumulation of detail. Nothing is more disheartening for a reader than the quotation of what is said to be amusing, deprived of the context which builds up the necessary tension ; but the following extract, chosen as much as anything for its brevity, illustrates the method. It occurs towards the end of the book : Jim Dixon is trying to catch a train on which will travel the girl he is in love with, and he can only do the journey in a maddeningly slow double-decker bus. The reader's sympathies are entirely with Dixon, and one shares his anxieties. There have been a number of delays. It is the kind of predicament every one has been in. Yet another delay occurs, when a farm tractor gets across the road.

Dixon thought he really would have to run down-stairs and knife the drivers of both vehicles; what next? what next? What actually would be next: a masked hold-up, a smash, floods, a burst tyre, an electric storm with falling trees and meteorites, a diversion, a low-level attack by Communist air-craft, sheep, the driver stung by a hornet? He'd choose the last of these, if consulted. Hawking its gears, the bus crept on, while every few yards troupes of old men waited to make their quivering way aboard.

(Chapter 24)

This is simple humour, but delightfully funny, and brilliantly written. The incongruity arises out of the clash of realism and fantasy, or realism and exaggeration, based on strong feeling of sympathetic frustration; and practically all the humour in the book, whether verbal or in the description of action, has the same basis. Thus the scene of the book is a provincial English university. The place is realistically though sketchily described. The characters also have a realistic basis. Apart from Dixon himself, the chief character is Professor Welch who is the head of Dixon's department. He is a stock English comic character, dear to a rather feeble lower-class type of humour, ' the absent-minded professor '. He is refurbished with some characteristically realistic traits (for example, he is not quite so foolish as he looks and he is something of a fraud). He has a firm real-istic base, but he is chiefly treated as a figure of farce. His unpleasant son, Bertrand, is even more farcically treated. The conflicts between Welch and Dixon are all farcically exaggerated.

The force of the book, however, lies in Dixon, the

incompetent new lecturer in medieval history. Dixon is on probation, hates his subject, and being particularly anxious to impress, does a number of childishly foolish and embarassing things, especially in the early part of the book. The success of the book lies in the extent to which the reader can associate himself with Dixon and his attitudes. The book's huge sales indicate that very many readers can easily so associate themselves.

Dixon represents an interesting combination of what are nowadays two very common situations, unusually closely linked. It is the linking which gives them force. The first is personal, the second social. The personal situation is one that must have been common to the English cultural pattern of all but the highest class for a long time: it is the unease and shyness of the late adolescent on first fully entering adult society. It is the kind of situation which makes us in such circumstances overset our teacup at the kind of tea-party we are not quite accustomed to attend. What makes this personal situation more acutely felt is the present social situation. For many young men nowadays the tea-party is given by someone of slightly higher social class than the one his family belongs to. Dixon's parents, though barely mentioned, are clearly far less well educated than he is. He is a university graduate, and education and social class are very closely linked in England.

The theme of *Lucky Jim* is Dixon's conflict with Welch on a professional, cultural and social level. It is important that Welch is socially and culturally, as well as professionally, superior to Dixon. (He is also financially superior, and it is part of the book's charm that no-one thinks or cares anything for that.   Money is not important.)

But Dixon's social ineptitude and personal embarassment are only the beginning of the story : the middle and end tell the story of Dixon's triumph over Welch, told with delightful verve and a fresh, vigorous comic invention.   At the beginning we, or at any rate very many English people, can easily identify ourselves with Dixon.   He is the awkward, bumbling ass we all feel ourselves to be, the impostor we all feel ourselves to be. And he represents all the very many people who have been educated into the kind of society they were not born into, a society where people know about Elizabethan music and modern art, as Dixon's parents, for example, do not.   But as the story proceeds Dixon changes—it is the novel's weakness and its delight.   There is no psychological interest, or knowledge, or development of character—very English in this.   But Dixon becomes a hero.   He knocks down Bertrand and honourably wins Bertrand's girl.   He defies the Welch's socially in various comical ways.   He loses his job, but gets a better one though at the same salary, as secretary to an eccentric millionaire.   He shows extraordinary ingenuity.   He can deal extremely effectively with impudent and patronising waiters in posh hotels.   This hardly agrees with his character at the beginning, but the very weakness of psychological insight is a strength here ; the question of inconsistency of character is never asked.   For we now identify ourselves even more enthusiastically with Dixon.   What seems to be superior culture has been discovered to be (according to the book) absurd pretentiousness. Dixon is now the adroit, clever, witty fellow we all feel ourselves to be. He can even make serious remarks about university teaching, quietly condemning the whole method of his seniors, and implying he could do much better if he were allowed to. He is the man we all feel ourselves to be, whose merit the world neglects, but whom anybody of real importance with a true idea of worth spots in a minute as being far better than these other, senior people. As the millionaire says of Dixon, other people have more qualifications, but we are subtly free from disqualifications.

Moreover, Dixon has real virtues. He has, in the second part of the book (not the first: the division comes where he spirits the heroine away from a dreary dance in another man's taxi) real courage, real cleverness, real good sense. He is also honest, decent, chaste and goodnatured. He will not tell the nasty truth about Bertrand in order merely to win a selfish personal advantage with the heroine. Unlike any hero of a book by Lawrence, Waugh, Huxley, Greene and others of an earlier generation, there is no question of him seducing the heroine. In other words, he may fairly be regarded as a symbolic hero of the lower middle-class. (The middle classes have always been the guardians of morality: the lower classes cannot afford it, and the upper classes can afford to neglect it.) He reveals the discomfort at and distrust of a higher range of culture which the crisis of expansion is bringing into the notice of the lower-middle class. (What is also typical is that there is in Dixon little or no conscious class-consciousness, and of course no idea at all of class-warfare. And his girl, whom he will certainly marry, is almost certainly of slightly higher social class than he.)

From the point of view of the book's success, however, it is important to realise that although it is perfectly capable of sociological analysis on a realistic scale, it is also a folk-tale. Here again, we find the book's strength in its combination of realism and fantasy. Who does not recognise in Dixon the hero of the first of Grimm's tales, *The Golden Goose*?

> There was a man who had three sons. The youngest was called Dummling—which is much the same as Dunderhead, for all thought he was more than half a fool—and he was at all times mocked and ill-treated by the whole household.

Yet it was Dummling who by his perseverance, his kindness to the old man, his carefree lack of concern for the golden goose's commercial value, who won the princess. He won her by making her laugh, just as Dixon's first success with the heroine lies in making her laugh. And like Dixon, Dummling too made a fool of persons richer and more dignified than he, as well as of officious members of his own or lower classes.

With this comparison in mind it will be understood that I do not suggest that Dixon is an actual embodiment of any particular class of persons in society. (Least of all do I suggest that he has any close autobiographical relationship to Mr. Amis.) He represents certain trends and new situations, even because he is very largely a fantasy figure. Although the book has high merits, it is certainly not a great novel. Its great and deserved success derives from the combination of qualities of wish-fulfillment and the exploration of a particular new social situation. When in years to come the social situation changes, the book will probably be found less fascinating than it now is.

It helped to release, however, a new type of hero, or at any rate a hero rather new to English fiction ; usually, like the hero of John Osborne's *Room at the Top*, they are far less attractive and decent than Dixon.

Lucky Jim's success as a novel has been equalled on the stage by John Osborne's *Look Back in Anger* (1956). Mr. Osborne is a professional actor in his late twenties, of whose background and education I know nothing. So far as I know he has never been associated with Mr. Amis, and his play provides some interesting similarities and contrasts with the novel.

What distinguishes him is passion, which is otherwise curiously deficient in the writing of the nineteen fifties. The play centres on the hero Jim Porter, a graduate of a provincial university, who in a most improbable way makes a poor living selling sweets. He is married to a girl of a rather higher social level and the play deals with his unpleasant treatment of his wife and his whining, self-pitying complaints against her, her family, and indeed the whole order of society. The play is in essence a monologue of complaint, though the two or three other characters concerned are well enough realised, and the rather irritating wife with her patient good will, is especially well drawn. This brief description will not make the play seem pleasant : it is not. Furthermore, the rather improbable social situation is matched

by the somewhat absurdly old-fashioned political ideas
that are expressed or implied. Jim Porter seriously
considers the British Royal Family to be a set of tyrants,
he is riddled with class-hostility, and he considers the
working-classes down-trodden. Especially since the
Labour Government of 1945–50 these ideas and attitudes
need serious modification, though of course they have
been long familiar to the British public, whether accepted or not. But his play has appealed to very many
people who obviously do not accept his ideas. (Who
can seriously think the Queen a tyrant?) What is the
source of his appeal? It is passion, and moreover, although his ideas are somewhat naive and old-fashioned,
his passion is modern. It is especially the passion of
frustration. The hero is himself a neurotic who is
not presented in sufficient depth for us fully to understand the roots of his neurosis, yet we share his passion.
The external circumstances of the plot are unconvincing,
as is much of the hero's character—for example, his
supposed attractiveness to women. But the tones in
which he speaks, the kind of remarks he makes, are
powerfully convincing. His fearful and maddened
confusion of thought and feeling, his self-pitying frustration, although exaggerated by art, express and help to
define a wide-spread mood, which has never been so
generally felt in England as it is today.

Mr. Osborne has marvellously caught the modern
version of Romantic rebellion. Rebellion is always a
necessary part of the mind, at least of the European
mind, and of the profoundly dualistic European temper.
Frustration arises nowadays, however, because paradoxi-

cally there seems little to rebel against, especially according to the old-fashioned political conventions of Mr. Osborne's thought (which naturally are those of the British public at large). Something seems wrong and there is a feeling of rebellion : in the old days it was possible to assert that the social system was wrong because it distributed benefits unequally ; but nowadays so simple a view is impossible to anyone with any consideration. There is still plenty wrong with the social system, but as is often remarked, there are no ' causes ' in the old social sense. It is plainly absurd, for example, to think of ' the working class ' (in itself nowadays a most dubious category of thought) as being down-trodden. It is absurd to think of the Queen as a tyrant. No wonder there is a sense of frustration. Something is wrong, but when we lash out at the old enemies they are dwindled to shadows.

This is another aspect of the crisis of expansion and of the attempts by education and material benefits to relieve it. New feelings are forced to use old ideas and conventions. Frustration arises when the new wine breaks the old bottles. The new feelings arise mainly from the changing social situation. For most people in England traditional beliefs of many kinds have broken down. On the other hand, employment is reasonably secure and no-one need starve. Material survival is assured. But because life at this level is easy it is also dull, and there is a natural thirst for stimulation, colour, interest, which may easily become, in Wordsworth's words, outrageous and degrading. For those, like Mr. Osborne, for whom this situation is

not good enough, anger and frustration are as natural
a response as is the original thirst for excitement arising
from dull safe jobs in dull ugly cities.

Both Jim Dixon and Jim Porter respond to the dis-
content with the present state of internal affairs in Great
Britain by attempting to escape. This is the more
curious because both their authors support the Labour
Party whose policies have brought about the present
distribution of material benefits, including education.
Each hero is a product of the crisis of expansion, in that
each has received a university education at a cost far
beyond anything his parents' income could have afforded.
Lucky Jim despises the level of society which his education has brought him into contact with, (though he
is in love with a girl from that level of society,) and
contracts out of a normal job to take a unique position
in the service of a millionaire—and the Welfare State
is bound to attempt to destroy millionaires. Jim Porter
has already married a girl of a superior social class, which
he has been qualified to enter by his education. Like
Lucky Jim, though far more frantically, Porter is acutely
uncomfortable in his relations with this higher level,
and savagely condemns it in and through his wife and
her family. The similarity of the social pattern in the
two works, separated so widely in tone and effect as
they are, is very noticeable.

The sense of frustration, however, is not purely social
or political. It has wider bases than either. The social
dilemma, though more acute and more widespread nowadays, has long existed without these results. The
underlying causes are more to do with the accumulated

effects of the decay of moral and spiritual conventions which only in the last thirty years has become really widespread. (In 1900, for example, most English people went to church : in 1950 most did not.)   Dixon's desire for escape, like Porter's hysterical anger, are signs of spiritual hunger.   They have no sense of purpose in life, such as is provided by Communism or Christianity or such personal faiths as some have worked out for themselves from the detritus of these two major faiths. Dixon and Porter have even passed beyond that last phase of religious belief, militant or self-conscious atheism.   They are not anti-religious because it has never occurred to either of them that anything could be said in favour of religion.   Dixon retains a personal morality unsupported by rational principles and apparently untested by reflection.   Porter retains a political morality of a sort, equally irrational, and not extending as far as personal behaviour.

Frustration occurs in Porter because he is more passionate and because for all his self-pity and self-indulgence he does have some power of mental generalisation which that least intellectual of men, Jim Dixon, apparently lacks.   Dixon avoids frustration largely because of his simpler temperament and superior luck ; but his amusing habit of making private faces is clearly a sign of frustration which unhappier and unluckier circumstances might well have developed.   In neither case has the hero any understanding of the true nature of his frustration.

The metaphysical situation of these heroes, though clear enough from a process of deduction, is not faced in the work of either Mr. Amis or Mr. Osborne.   It is uncovered and made plain in an extremely good poem by Philip Larkin, the third representative writer I have chosen.

Philip Larkin is of similar age and background to Mr. Amis, and is also a member of St. John's College, Oxford, where he associated with Kingsley Amis and with another talented and representative critic, poet and novelist, John Wain.   Philip Larkin is now a University Librarian.

The poem is *Church Going*, written in the first person, though the person who is speaking is no more to be confused with Mr. Larkin himself than Dixon with Mr. Amis or Porter with Mr. Osborne.   The speaker in the poem is recognisably brother to Dixon and Porter, though less lively than the one, less neurotic than the other, less assertive than either.   He describes himself looking round in an old church

> *Bored, uninformed, knowing the ghostly silt*
> *Dispersed*, yet tending to this cross of ground
> Through suburb scrub because it held unspilt
> So long and equably what since is found
> Only in separation—marriage, and birth,
> And death, and thoughts of these—for whom was built
> This special shell?   *For, though I've no idea*
> *What this accoutred frowsty barn is worth*,
> It pleases me to stand in silence here;
>
> A serious house on serious earth it is,
> In whose blent air all our compulsions meet,
> Are recognised, and robed as destinies.
> And that much never can be obsolete,

Since someone will forever be surprising
A hunger in himself to be more serious,
And gravitating with it to this ground,
Which, he once heard, was proper to grow wise in,
If only that so many dead lie round.

(*Italics mine.*)

The speaker in the poem is, like both Dixon and Porter, ignorant of the general cultural tradition; a little embarassed by its evidences; contemptuous; and very little interested. Among these traditions are of course the cultural activities of the arts, and also religious faith and a conception of purpose in life described as ' ghostly silt '.

The poet sees more deeply than the speaker, his *persona*. The *persona*, this third Jim, is hardly one who is capable of such subtle self-analysis as is found throughout the poem. It is the poet who (unlike the novelist or the playwright) notes the ' hunger to be more serious ' as a part of the *persona*. The Dixon of the second part of *Lucky Jim* is not without seriousness, and Jim Porter has only too much, but they do not recognise in themselves the kind of hunger which it is one of the aims of *Church Going* throughout its length to define, and which is a common product of the crisis of expansion. Probably Philip Larkin's recognition of this hunger, no longer to be defined by the conventions of political thought, is what saves him from the maddened frustration of *Look Back in Anger* and the seeds of frustration scattered here and there in *Lucky Jim*. The catch-phrase ' Angry Young Man ', first applied to Mr. Osborne's play, has been all too widely applied.   It does not apply to the work of Mr. Amis and Mr. Larkin, nor to the work of a number of other writers who might be associated with them.

Church Going is remarkably central to the present cultural and literary situation. It shows the break with tradition, and the uneasy relationship to tradition, accompanied by embarassment, ignorance, contempt, and sense of loss. It springs from a lower middle class expansion of educational opportunities, and explores a lower middle class world, just as *Lucky Jim* and *Look Back in Anger* do. The rest of Mr. Larkin's poems, gathered together in *The Less Deceived* (1955), explore and reveal further aspects of that world. To very many readers in England today they are met with instant recognition—*this is my world, too*. It is a world of the provinces, rather than of London; of day-schools, not public schools; of ordinary people unconnected with those who run the country : a notable contrast with the world of the Bloomsbury group, or of the characteristic writers of the nineteen-thirties, the world described so well by Stephen Spender in *World within World*. The poem *I Remember, I Remember* is a deliberate contrast to the golden childhoods of many of the dominant writers of the first half of the twentieth century. The poet describes stopping in a train at the station of his home town, Coventry :

> ' Was that ', my friend smiled, ' where you " have your
>   roots " ? '
> No, only where my childhood was unspent,
> I wanted to retort, just where I started :
> By now I've got the whole place clearly charted.

> Our garden, first: where I did not invent
> Blinding theologies of flowers and fruits,
> And wasn't spoken to by an old hat.
> And here we have that splendid family
>
> I never ran to when I got depressed
> The boys all biceps and the girls all chest . . .
>
> 'You look as if you wished the place in Hell',
> My friend said, 'judging from your face.' 'Oh well,
> I suppose it's not the place's fault,' I said.
>
> 'Nothing, like something, happens anywhere.'

The irony and wit, the colloquial directness, the honesty, the almost excessive distrust of pretentiousness are very characteristic, as is the homeliness of the subject-matter and the diction. Rebelliousness is also there, but it is immediately checked by a sense of balance and proportion which is also found in *Lucky Jim* and which is so singularly lacking, for good and ill, in *Look Back in Anger*. Rebelliousness, similarly checked, is found in several other poems. There is also in other poems a perception, the more effective for the unsentimental restraint of its portrayal, of the suffering of the world, the groaning of creation, which the poet describes untouched by self-pity, or even by a sense of personal suffering. Suffering is represented as arbitrary, the product of the arbitrary, essentially accidental, nature of the whole of existence. And with this view of existence goes an intense awareness of the value and loss of time, and of death as the end of all.

With Larkin's poems we escape into a wider world of perception than is felt in *Lucky Jim* or *Look Back in*

Anger because we are brought again into a consideration
of the human situation. In so doing we can see the
crisis of expansion as something more important than
the emancipation of however vast a class of men. There
are other considerations than the merely social. The
failure of traditional culture is not simply that it cannot
be grafted within one generation upon a whole forest
of new social saplings. The failure is an actual failure
of traditional culture to meet the challenges of modern
science and tenchnology sufficiently quickly. (This
makes the situation one of great interest to Japan, where
the same crisis, at the moment not quite so advanced,
is rapidly developing.) To take only one representative
example, it is clear that in England traditional Christianity can never regain the hold it once had. At an intellectual level the developments, begun in the nineteenth
century, of scientific and psychological discoveries,
demand the abandonment of many traditional concepts : at a cultural level the language of Bible and
Prayer Book is practically incomprehensible to the ordinary man : at a social level, the geography of the parish
and the requirement of Sunday church-going crumble
before rapid transportation and week-end motoring.
If Christianity is to survive it must change in many
ways and it shows few signs of doing so. One sees it
occasionally implied that the attitude represented by the
persona Dixon, Porter, and the speaker in *Church Going*,
is culpably ignorant and boorish. Few would deny
(least of all, no doubt, their creators) that such *personae*
are sadly lacking in breadth of out-look, sense of purpose, personal grace. But they respond honestly and

energetically to what they perceive of the world which has in large measure created them. If they fail traditional culture, it is because traditional culture has first failed them.

It is worth noting that although the creators of Dixon, Porter and the rest have no doubt much in common with their *personae*, they are not in every respect like them. Dixon threw up his job at the University, or at any rate, behaved in such a way as naturally to lose it, but Mr. Amis has had no difficulty in retaining his. Mr. Osborne is not paralyzed by frustration. These writers tend to write of persons less talented, socially more humble, than themselves.

There is also more conformity in the books than might at first have been suspected in view of the unquestionable boredom with and desire to escape from normal society. Mr. Osborne is the least conforming, but he is also the least intellectual, the most simple-minded and passionate, of the three. The Dixon of the second part of *Lucky Jim* is capable of understanding and discriminating within systems of some complexity, and in no case shows a desire to upset society. He is the mildest of reformers in his final comments on teaching history in a university, for all his fun at the expense of the elderly and the established. Mr. Larkin shows no social interests at all, but has an ironic appreciation of the complications and tangles within the individual human temperament, which prevents him from being simple-minded about anything. Furthermore all three show a desire to communicate with a wide audience which is in itself a desire for conformity and agreement. Whatever their view of society, they are not didactic on the one hand, nor revolutionary in technique and careless of being understood, on the other. (Passionate didacticism is the reaction of the conservative, obscurity is the reaction of the revolutionary, in literary matters.) In technique *Lucky Jim* is an old-fashioned novel, easily understood by ordinary people. Forster, Joyce, Lawrence, Virginia Woolf, might never have written for all their effect upon it. Mr. Larkin's poems are subtler, there is nothing simple about them—except their appearance. Clarity is one of his aims. He uses such homely imagery as the bubble that forms at the end of a dripping tap, a picture of old race-horses. He speaks colloquially, uses slang—in a word, makes no attempt to stand apart from his audience. Mr. Osborne in technique does not differ much from his predecessors in realistic drama. His ideas are old-fashioned, well established enough to be widely familiar, whether agreed or disagreed with.

Along with this conformity to the audience goes a certain narrowness. One is reminded of Dickens, his lack of philosophy, his ignorance of so much traditional culture and of foreign achievements. None of these present writers have anything like Dickens's greatness or his ignorance of the past and of foreign culture, but the similarity is there. (We also have in Mr. Eliot our contemporary Arnold, preaching ' Europeanness '.) Unlike earlier twentieth-century poets, Mr. Larkin shows no sign of foreign influences. The hero of *Look Back in Anger* appears to have no international views, although his father had died as a result of the Spanish

Civil War.   There are similarly no apparent intellectual or artistic influences from within England at work in these writers. Philosophy, science, religion, music, art make no contribution, though the last three are held up to ridicule in *Lucky Jim*.   No-one ever reads a book, though Porter despises the only two respectable Sunday newspapers in England.

This leads to the final point : which is a reminder, of what the reader will already be conscious of, that although these three writers are the most representative writers of the present day as far as we can easily judge, they are in no way totally representative.   In England today science and philosophy still flourish and there is if anything a ' renaissance ' in English art, and perhaps in music too.   If religion does not flourish it is still fairly strong.   There are besides scores of novelists who are more than competent, and one or two, like William Golding, who are extremely good.   There are few successful playwrights, but many plays are written. There are also dozens of good poets.   There are travel-writers, essayists, critics.   But there can be no doubt that the *general* temper of the day, and the essential situation, is better represented by the writers I have discussed than by any others.   Perhaps it is inevitable in the present situation that literature is rather less in-clusive of the general culture of the country today than it has been at certain times in the past.

The crisis of expansion shows no sign of working it-self out yet, and there are many reasons why it is difficult for a work of literature to reflect so difficult and varied a world.   Some narrowing of scope is perhaps inevitable. But there is also an advance: new levels of society, new kinds of people, and in some cases new states of feeling, new attitudes of mind, are being explored by contemporary writers with honesty, energy, amusement, sometimes passion. These are more important than trivial experiments with technique, carried out merely for the sake of novelty, which are usually associated with the idea of an *avant-garde* of literature.

Contemporary literature, in the representatives I have discussed and in others, is not stagnant: it is lively, unpretentious, interesting. The false and the inflated are attacked with a moral zeal that may be joyous or bitter. When one compares these writers with earlier English writers one is bound to notice how characteristically English they are. Their technique is conservative: their view of character has hardly changed since Chaucer's time: they are individualistic and yet chiefly interested in the social scene. Some earlier traits in English literature are little noticeable, but the general temper, the general mode of approaching reality, is astonishingly comparable with the general characteristics of the long centuries that have gone before.

PROTEUS (ブルーワー文学論集)

昭和 33 年 7 月 25 日　印　　　　刷
昭和 33 年 7 月 30 日　初 版 発 行
昭和 41 年 7 月 31 日　初版第 2 刷発行

著　者　　D. S. Brewer
発行者　　小　酒　井　益　蔵
　　　　　(東京都新宿区神楽坂 1 の 2)
印刷所　　研究社印刷株式会社
　　　　　(東京都新宿区神楽坂 1 の 2)

発行所　　研究社出版株式会社
　　　　　東京都新宿区神楽坂 1 の 2
　　　　　振替口座　東京 83761 番

定価　￥300